Surprised by Imperfection

SHARI BRAND RAY

Bohannon Hall Press

Printed in the United States of America
First Edition

Library of Congress Control Number: 2022912574

Publisher's Cataloging-in-Publication Data

Ray, Shari Brand, 1960-
Surprised by imperfection: Essays and stories on Wonder / by Shari Brand Ray ; illustrated by Sarah Robin Coleman.
Niceville, FL: Bohannon Hall Press, 2022.
299 p.: illustrations ; 18 cm.
First edition.

1. Ray, Shari Brand—Literary collections. 2. Literary Collections—Essays. 3. Biography & Autobiography – Personal Memoirs. I. Title. II. Coleman, Sarah Robin, 1977-
PS3618.A9 S87 2022 2022912574

ISBN 979-8-9850298-2-6 (softcover)

Published by Bohannon Hall Press

To Nanny and Geezer
for everything

There is no exquisite beauty . . .
without some strangeness in the proportion.

Edgar Allan Poe

Glory be to God for dappled things.

Gerard Manley Hopkins

Author's Note

A young colleague recently asked me why I waited so long to write a book. My quick answer was, "I have no idea," but the truer answer is that I've been writing this book for over twenty-five years. The stories in this collection are about Antwerp, Belgium, where we lived and loved for a while, and teaching English in high school where I still live and love, stories about my dear father's battle with Parkinson's and dementia, and stories about my different little left hand. Stories about family and love and love lost and the stars and the moon and heartbreak and forgiveness and the lack thereof.

Twenty-five years of writing story after story.

Then one day, not long ago, my friend Sheila read some Advent pieces I wrote and connected me with a brilliant publisher who asked, "Could you send me a couple of your essays?" I did, and then he asked, "Could you send a few more?" And this book was born.

Sometimes it seems like people are sitting around just waiting for the birth of a new thing, but what is actually happening is that they are working with all their might preparing for birth in faith, without knowing the birth date – enduring birth pangs with patience until the time is right. And then, finally, hope is realized and the time is right, and something new and good is born.

Such is the way of things here on this lovely planet of ours.

Table of Contents

AUTUMN

Surprised by Imperfection

She was only nineteen, he twenty-two, when the rabbit died and the young couple found out they were expecting their first baby. Married for a mere year and some change, my parents had recently moved from a medium-sized town in buggy, steamy central Mississippi to the equally hot and river-humid, sticky-hot big-city of Memphis, Tennessee, with the dogged hope and determined dreams of the young.

My father had been recruited by Premier Fastener to sell industrial bolts and screws and nuts and washers on 100% sales commission which, for a shy man, was a daunting proposition, although not as daunting as hunger. And since a baby was on her way, my mother had not yet found a job and was unavailable for job-searching for the immediate future. My father's first job in Memphis did not pay much – it took him a decade or two to become salesman enough to branch out on his own – but it was a start and it was not pumping gas in Hattiesburg. They made rent, albeit just barely, thank God turnip greens and cornbread were cheap, and every other weekend they drove the six-hours in his 1955 Hillman from Memphis to Decatur to visit his family and, equally important, to load up two silver ice chests with frozen vegetables from

Papaw's vast backyard garden and beef from his cows.

It was a fine, good start.

While the first sonogram dates back to 1958, for a normal patient in the early days of the 1960's there was no knowing the gender of a baby *in utero*, a fact that added even more excitement to the day. No ultra-sounds or 4-D imaging for these kids, no gender-hints, just good, old-fashioned waiting. Babies were showered in neutral colors while their mothers waited out their many months, watched for the pains to begin, then hands-on-bellies shuffled off to the hospital where the mother labored until the doctor administered a general anesthesia and she fell into a twilight sleep, calming her travail and leaving the doctor in charge of the birth. And most of the time things went along just fine.

My father sat alone in the waiting room as my soon-to-be grandparents had not yet arrived from the country. We'll get there as soon as we can, we're packing up now, they said on the phone. So my spanking-new-father had no hand to hold when the serious, stony-faced doctor arrived, his mouth fixed and grim with difficult news.

There's an issue, the doctor said in a hushed and practiced tone, can you come with me?

My father heard a voice unexpected.

A quiet man as well as a meek one, my father nodded and walked down the hospital corridors a few steps behind the equally reticent obstetrician. Their silent heads leaned downward, the two men stopped at the nursery window for a first look at the new baby, perfect in every way, except for her tiny left arm that curved back so sharply at the elbow, and her little three-fingered hand that nearly touched her shoulder, like a teardrop.

We don't know why these things happen sometimes, the gentle doctor began, his voice low. My father told me later the doctor's words sounded distant in his ears, ringing like deep echoes rising up from the well on his grandmother's farm.

Does the baby's mother know about this? my father mumbled his only question, trying to get his mind around the phenomenon, watching the sleeping infant who had no idea her little imperfect arm bent back so far or that parts of her were missing.

No, the doctor replied. Mother is still sleeping.

My mother woke from her twilight slumber soon enough, and as the story goes, my parents walked those hushed steps to the hospital nursery together to first-hold their new baby and wonder how in the world things like this work out. They talked to the doctors and cried and feared and prayed and marveled and cried again and eventually took their stolid steps toward peace.

But for a solitary moment, my precious twenty-two-year-old father, who had just taken an intimidating new job and moved from the only town he'd ever known, now stood alone in the big-city with his infant daughter resting behind the thick glass wall of the hospital nursery and all he could do was gaze at her little teardrop arm, slightly raised, and wonder.

Not too long ago I spoke with my father about the particulars of our story. We were having lunch at the Subway in the Abraham Lincoln Museum in Springfield, Illinois – which I highly recommend, both the museum and its sandwiches – and I asked my father to remember about that time. He had just been diagnosed with Parkinson's disease, and I was gathering facts and listening to stories and asking questions and throwing it into a journal as fast as I could before his memory faded.

We all were.

I was interested in what had popped into his head during those quiet first moments at the hospital. He smiled at my question. As he recalled, his first thoughts were not about my little hand-and-arm at all, but rather he claimed his first thought was 'How am I *ever* going to be able to take care of these two girls, with nothing but a crummy old Hillman almost too small to fit us all in. I work on commission; I'm making no money. If I pay the $57.50 for rent then we don't have enough food and if I pay for food, I can't afford gasoline and our little house has only one window unit air conditioner to keep us cool in these brutal summers so I sweat all night long and can't sleep. I wonder how any of this will ever work out.'

But of course, it did. For after all the crying, there is still life waiting to be lived. My brand-new parents gathered their wits and listened and talked and prayed their prayers and asked their questions to all the pediatricians and orthopedic docs that paraded through their lives for the next days and months, ever more questions than answers: Surgery? Braces? Physical therapy? Prostheses? Come back in two weeks, come back in six weeks, we'll need to see her routinely for a while.

We did not have money for any of those shenanigans, my father reported at lunch, sipping at his Coke.

Finally, a doctor-prophet walked into their lives somewhere around my twelfth week, a soon-to-be-retiring orthopedic sage who took a long bespectacled look at this baby girl's little curved arm with its stiff little three-fingered hand. He touched her teardrop arm gently, bending, pressing, stretching, eyeballing, and then looked the young parents square in their eager, frightened faces and simply said, Don't spend any more of your money at this clinic. Go home, and let her grow up, then buy this child some skates and teach her to turn a cartwheel.

Which is exactly what they did.

I have no memory of these events nor of the strength of my parents in those first days of having a child with a physical disability. My memories begin a bit later, years filled with miraculous ordinary moments.

Like the afternoon I came home after just a few days into the first grade with a question on my lips, a simple question for my mother that needed a direct, factual answer, and I am blessed with a mother skilled at direct, factual answers.

Mama, am I crippled?

She paused but only for a moment. I wonder now that I've raised a daughter of my own if my mother had not been anticipating this moment or if she really was this good on her feet?

Who taught you that word? my mother queried.

Carl McCoy.

Hmm, Carl, she whispered to herself. Well, first let me ask you this. Is there anything you want to do that you cannot do if you put your mind to it?

Nope, I said with the grand conviction of an undaunted six-year-old.

Well, then you're not crippled. And don't say that word anymore.

Easy enough.

Mama, I *am* having some trouble with my cartwheel, I offered, wondering if that fact was enough to qualify a short-armed girl as crippled.

Then go outside and keep practicing, my mother said as she turned from me to fetch the potatoes out of the oven.

With my mother, it really was as simple as that.

I recall ordinary moments when having a strange little hand was an important something to consider.

The moment when Lou Banks looked me hard in the face and said, I will help you, but if you want to learn to play the piano, you will have to work twice as hard as everyone else. You must learn to play notes with your right hand that your left hand can't reach, and you must practice harder and longer than my other students to achieve the same success. I will accept nothing from you but your very best.

I can do that.

And I remember Lou Banks, six years later, sitting on the front row when I won the high school talent contest playing Scott Joplin's "The Entertainer," fair and square.

And that time when Mrs. McPherson repeated Lou Banks' admonition almost word for word: I will help you, but if you really want to learn to type, you will have to work harder than everyone else. You must learn a different set of home keys and your right hand will have to do the lion's share of the work. Don't sign up for this class unless you plan on working really hard. I will not accept anything from you but your very best.

I can do that.

I remember Mrs. Mac's wink and grin at the end-of-the-year awards ceremony when I did *not* win the Typing Award, but she and I both knew I had come in a very close second. And that day senior year she kept me after class and called to my attention a habit I'd perfected without realizing it – keeping my little hand stuffed into my back pocket, hidden from sight.

You're beautiful, she said gently, just the way you are. You should never hide your beauty, now take your hand out of your pocket.

So, I did.

People who require from us our very best are an unspeakable gift.

I remember the moment my own three-year-old daughter first noticed my hand, taking my little hand into her own and kissing and stroking and loving and exclaiming, I love little hand! I can't wait to get to Heaven because in Heaven I'll have a little hand just like yours.

I suppose it goes without saying that not everyone finds physical differences beautiful. People can be thoughtless and too often cruel. The lower school playground is *not* for the faint of heart. Neither is the middle school cafeteria. When a young child has to learn to balance her school lunch plate on the back of her three-fingered hand, there will be spills.

It isn't easy to learn to live imperfectly. There are voices who say, Ew, don't touch me with those three fingers and your hand looks like a dinosaur and that's so weird and aren't you going to get that hand fixed? People who stare, and worse, people who look away. People whose parents didn't teach them about compassion and empathy, about beauty in imperfection and strength in weakness; perhaps because no one taught them.

Difficult words can be as important as lovely, easy words, maybe more so. In these moments when we are reminded of our collective human weakness, we can hear God speak through the multitude of voices – My power is made perfect in weakness.

We don't know why these things happen sometimes, the gentle doctor said to my scared young father in the earliest moments of my life, and those words rang distant to him then, like echoes of old fears.

My new-father was fearful of the unfamiliar, scared of the vocabulary of the unknown. He was surprised by imperfection.

But he learned to listen to the other voices. The sage words of the wise and the strong and the compassionate, voices that dispel fear rather than encourage it. Hopeful, loving voices that calm and reassure and say things like, Don't spend any more of your money at this clinic. Go home, let her grow up, let her live her life. Let her learn her way to skate and type and turn cartwheels and cheer and play the piano and swim.

I'm learning to listen to the voices of grace that reveal the beauty in the imperfection rather than in spite of it.

De Bruintjes

It's always hard to be the new girl, but this little one was starting out with two real strikes against her. She was beginning school in the middle of the year, it was already the end of October, and she didn't speak the language, not a single word. She was a foreigner.

We had just moved to Antwerp, Belgium, and were living in a tiny, furnished apartment in the *Fruithoflaan*. The *Fruithoflaan* boasted of ultra-chic shopping and tulip-laden bicycle parks, and the street was filled with carts and vendors hawking the culinary wares of the season – apples, pears, cherries, and lots and lots of potatoes – twice-cooked Belgian *fritjes* became an immediate staple. We came to rely on the rotisserie-chicken truck parked outside of our apartment building every afternoon, the name "Chicken-Boy Chicken" emblazoned in red flames across its girth.

The *Fruithoflaan* is a street not to be missed.

This was a temporary address for us, though. We would stay in the *Fruithoflaan* through our language learning and then move to downtown Antwerp. The container carrying our household goods sat on the dock until we established a more permanent residence, so, for those early eight months we lived with what we carried with us on the plane – coats and scarfs, books and Barbies, and lots of black clothing. It was enough and we were not ungrateful for excitement and adrenaline alone carried us through the adventures of the first months until our container arrived.

Yet, despite the quaintness of our new city and the beauty of our already-beloved *Fruithoflaan,* I felt transient; I had never before experienced the odd feeling of living *here* while my household things were over *there.* It, and I, felt foreign.

We decided to put our second-grade daughter into a national school. Thankfully our employers had already scouted out a few Dutch schools before we arrived, so my first-week agenda was predominated by visiting these schools and trying to make a good decision when I really didn't know what-the-heck was going on. But, as I said, it was already the end of October, so the sooner the better.

After two well-translated but abysmal school visits – one school director actually said, we have to accept her because it's the law, but we cannot give her any extra help with her language learning, I can tell you that for sure. We simply have too many foreigners here! – we arrived at the last school on the list. I felt some real pressure to like this one, not only because the other two had been so unfriendly, but this little neighborhood school was just a block off the *Fruithoflaan,* so we could walk. I wanted this to happen.

The *Directrice* of the school was slightly late for our meeting and thus she bumbled and fumbled her delightful way through stacks of papers on her desk to find our information.

Hello and it is nice to meet you, she said in English.

Nice to meet you as well, I replied, hand outstretched. She took my hand and pumped it energetically, eager-eyed, smiling, and then turned to my translator and blurred into a wave of gesticulation, articulation, and laughter. This *Directrice* was a happy woman, one that made others happy by just being around her, a rare breed indeed. I didn't even care that she was arranging our new life with words I couldn't understand. I wanted Rainey to be at this school, guided through by this *Directrice.*

The appointment ended with successful understanding and three Flemish kisses on cheeks. We agreed on a starting day – tomorrow! – so there was much work to be done. School supply shopping, booklets of lined paper for mathematics, a Hello Kitty book satchel, leather pencil case, and the obligatory fountain pen of all inky-fingered European school children.

The students at this girls' school wore uniforms, chocolate brown skirts and matching brown sweaters with pale peach blouses underneath. We had seen these little brown-clad girls skipping back and forth to school through the tulip park nearest our apartment on the *Fruithoflaan.* In the neighborhood they were called the *bruintjes,* "the little brown ones," or better "the dear brown ones," and Rainey and I were eager for her to become one.

Sleep often evades on the eve of something new.

The charming laughter of the *Directrice* must have been contagious because the morning schoolyard of the *bruintjes* was filled with the squeals of girls happy in their place. They were a busy lot that particular morning with ropes to jump and balls to bounce and jacks to toss and stories to tell. Eventually, lessons to learn.

Belgian schoolchildren address their teachers as *Juffrouw*, usually shortened to *Juf* (say the word "roof" but start it with a y, "yoof," heavy on the *f* at the end. Yes, that's it). We were not able to meet Rainey's *Juf* yesterday for she had been away on a field trip to the Antwerp Zoo. This morning, however, Rainey's *Juf* was on morning duty in the schoolyard, and my instructions from the *Directrice* had been crystal clear: find the *Juf* on the play yard and introduce yourself and Rainey. *Juf* speaks enough English for these introductions. Then you (she meant me) need to go home. We've had other non-Dutch speakers here before, and we know what we're doing. All will be well. So, bye-bye.

This was the moment I dreaded, stomach turning and hand shaking. Is this real?

The iron gate of the schoolyard stood slightly open, beckoning entrée for all *bruintjes.* Despite the sweet singing of jump rope songs beyond the gate, this was the moment I dreaded, stomach turning and hand shaking. Is this real? We stopped still, mother and daughter, just this side of the gate.

Am I actually taking her to a school where she doesn't even know how to ask about the restroom, can't read the homework sheet, or even say "hello" properly?

Am I going to leave her here with a *Juf* who teaches in another language? How will my daughter learn? Will I leave her here all day, in this new land with its customs which, albeit beautiful, we do not understand. Who does this?

Foreigners. We were the foreigners.

There are clichés for these moments: get out or get in, do or die, sink or swim. But in those real moments between sinking and actually beginning to swim, getting in when we'd rather be getting out, clichés fail and the earth falters a bit and one must find one's footing again.

So, I do what I have been told to do – such is my nature, for what it's worth. We passed through the iron school gate and entered the schoolyard, my seven-year-old daughter and me. I found the *Juf* at the head of the play yard and began to cough out my rehearsed introduction.

Now, this *Juf* was not what I'd expected. To the same degree the *Directrice* was personable and cute, almost giggly, the *Juf* was serious and unsmiling. She stood rocklike under the awning of the building, face hard-set, a large woman with a graying crew cut, arms crossed strong under her ample Belgian bosom; the *Juf* was also dressed in brown but not the cute chocolate brown of all the squealing *bruintjes* in the play yard. No, this was the austere dark beige of a prison guard, and her face matched her shirt – beige, a color devoid of emotion.

Is *that* the *Juf?* my seven-year-old peeped, waiting for her mother's assurance that things are as they should be.

Why yes, I think it is, I choked and stammered and squeaked out a miserable reply, nothing left of the earlier morning's joyful confidence. We were on our own. This was the big time.

It's like those times when you decide to bungee jump or sky dive or eat rattlesnake in Mexico or put on a virtual reality headset at a party. It seems like a great idea at the time until the moment comes to actually do it, and then you wonder *How did I get here?* and *Whose brilliant idea was this anyway?* Or when you feel compelled to whisper *I love you* to the companion strapped with you on the eight-story giant swing because you know down deep, this is it, the point from which you may not return.

When I realized Rainey and I had been standing stock-still for an indefinite period of time just inside the gate and in the midst of dozens and dozens of cheerful, brown-clad school children, I finally woke up and moved. We took meaningful steps toward the building, toward the *Juf,* and the closer we got, the bigger she got. Although she clearly saw us coming, she did not budge, neither did she blink. I couldn't decide if she was being territorial or whether she was simply allowing us to do all the moving. Either way, we took a few thin steps forward and found ourselves under the awning with her. The moment had arrived.

Good morning, I cough. I am Shari and this is Rainey, your new student. It's nice to meet you.

Ja.

The *Directrice* told us to meet you here today.

Ja.

We have purchased all the necessary supplies on the supply sheet, so I think she's ready to go.

Ja. The *Juf* looked up and caught my eye, and I thought I saw a flicker of kindness but I wasn't sure. The *Juf* most certainly had the home field advantage.

I am both a teacher and a parent, I know the importance of

good *mojo* between parent and school. That a child feels safe and cared for is of utmost importance to everyone. But this day, the problem was glaringly simple; neither the *Juf* nor I could say what we wanted to say. We had the desire; we simply did not have the vocabulary.

My heart would have to speak for me. I wondered if it was possible that my heart and the *Juf*'s spoke the same language even when our tongues did not?

Juffrouw, you know that this is my baby, right? My usual confidence wanes this morning. We've only been in Antwerp a few days, and she doesn't speak a single word of Dutch. She won't be able to read from the text for a while. I couldn't even tell her how to ask for a drink of water. I bought the cute brown uniform, so she looks like a bruintje, *but she isn't one yet, is she? Do you know I am a teacher, too, so I know exactly how much extra work you will have with a foreign student, and I'm both tremendously sorry and terrifically grateful. But I must be honest: if you were delightfully cute and smiley like the Directrice, I think this moment would be easier. But you are large and austere and, frankly, a bit scary. No offense, but I think it's the crew cut. Or the massive bosom, it's hard to know. Will you be gentle and patient with this new* bruintje? *My hands tremble, do I have reason to fear?*

At that moment the *Juf* uncrossed her arms and reached out to take her new student by the hand. Her large Flemish hand overtook the small American one and she drew Rainey in, nestling her new student securely into the folds of her ample self. The newest *bruintje* blinked her large green eyes several hard times as her tight, auburn ringlets were enveloped by the beige woman; no tears, mind you, but rather the wide-eyed wonder of a child who just realized she might be lost.

The *Juf* delivered her one single, rehearsed line, Don't *vorry*. Return at 3:00, wait at gate. Good bye.

And then there was one.

The bell rang and small platoons of well-trained *bruintjes* lined up and filed inside with Rainey and the *Juf* hand-in-hand leading the chocolate parade. They vanished inside the new school and I stood outside, by myself. The day had begun, there was much to learn – a new language, for one thing – and I had been dismissed. Someone closed the great iron gate of the schoolyard with a loud *bang* and it was finished. No parents allowed.

Don't *vorry*.

Sage advice in any language. In fact, I heard the birds on the *Fruithoflaan* singing those same lyrics as I walked the slow blocks through the park toward home. *Peace, be still*, they sang and danced, with *Fear not, I am with thee* as their next chorus, a reminder that if I cannot sing for joy in this moment, the birds and the rocks and the flowers and the trees will do it for me.

The school day passed deliberately. My husband and I ambled down the ancient cobbled streets of old Antwerp, we ate spicy pita *shoarma* from a Moroccan vendor, we visited the cathedral, *Onze-Lieve-Vrouwekathedraal*, which *wows* on regular days but this was no regular day.

I spent the day checking my watch, scattered and absent-minded and making the deliberate choice to worry. I didn't care about the birds' song. I didn't care that the *Juf*, whom I feared, and the *Directrice*, whom I trusted, had both assured me that all would be well. I chose to miss the beauty of the unusually mild October day in my wonderful new city and carried anxiety instead, a conscious decision, all day long until 3:00.

This is no way to live.

Needless to say, I was the first parent to arrive at the iron gate that afternoon for pick-up. The *bruintjes* were still inside hard at work, and I would have to wait a bit longer for the bell to ring and the school yard to fill again with noisy girls.

(I'm just glad I didn't embarrass myself by standing here with my hands on the bars of the gate all day long.)

Bruintjes come to school neat and tidy, their peach blouses tucked in tight and brown socks pulled up, but *Bruintjes* depart school disheveled and unkempt, ponytails fallen and sweaters stretched from playing and huge smiles – it appeared that *Bruintjes* spent their school days happy.

The newest *Bruintje* ran out the school doors grinning and skipping and shouting at her new friends in her new tongue:

Dag, Sophie! Dag, Maike! Ciao, vriendjes!

Tot ziens, Rainey! a couple of *Bruintjes* shouted their departures.

Tot ziens! the newest *Bruintje* shouted in reply.

I looked deep into those big, doe eyes for hints of fear and found none. I'm coming here again tomorrow, right, Mama? This is my new school, right? my daughter begged.

Yes, *Bruintje,* we will be back tomorrow.

Before we turned to go, the *Juf,* on afternoon duty as well, caught my eye. She had resumed her stalwart pose under the awning of the school, strong arms crossed hard beneath that great bosom. She unlocked them, though, when she saw me and gave a little grin and a little nod and an eager thumbs-up with both hands. A good sign in most languages, I suppose.

It is good, the *Juf* shouted across the yard. It will be good. Don't *vorry.*

Thanks, *Juf,* I shout back. I won't.

Both Paul and Jesus preached the *Juf*'s message, or perhaps I should say she preached theirs, all of these sages reminding me to be anxious for nothing. *Fear not.* How is it possible that I can forget the birds who neither toil nor spin while I watch their God feed and provide for them every day from my back porch perch? Do I ever really consider the lily?

Do I dare trust that if I seek first the kingdom of God, all these things will be added, even for me, a foreigner in a foreign land?

A strong woman told me not to *vorry,* and she was right.

Thanks, *Juf.* We'll see you tomorrow.

Turkey, Doritos, and Kibbles

On our first Thanksgiving together, Larry brought home a twenty-five-pound turkey. At that time, in the early 1980s, the Lynchburg Gas Company gifted all their employees a turkey for Thanksgiving and we were duly thankful for it, all *twenty-five pounds* of it. The problem was, of course, what to do with it. Back then we were two relatively skinny people with a new puppy named Brandy, and the three of us together simply could not eat that much turkey if we ate it on sandwiches and cooked it into casseroles from this Thanksgiving until the onset of the Apocalypse.

I would have frozen it, but our freezer was too small. I would have cooked it, sliced it up, and *then* frozen it, but our freezer was still too small. Everything in the duplex where we lived at 204½ Euclid Ave was too small; in fact, my tiny refrigerator itself barely had the space for this massive, formidable frozen beast to rest.

Larry had the idea, as he was so inclined, to invite people over for Thanksgiving who had no place to go. We were still in college and couldn't get off work to go home to Memphis for the holiday, and certainly there were plenty of others like us wandering aimlessly around empty dormitory hallways, a bit lonely and slightly homesick for dressing and turkey, of which, as it turned out, we now had plenty.

I'll go to the dorms and shout out for anyone who needs a place to go for Thanksgiving dinner, he said. I'll ask all the people at my work who are lonely to come, he said.

OK, I said. But we ourselves are quite poor, remember? You're working two jobs and going to school, and I'm student teaching and sneaking over to the mall to work evenings and weekends (I may or may not have agreed to the university's policy of student teachers not working outside jobs – my memory is murky on this point). How will we pay for the food for all the people who might show up? And, while we're at it, you know I've never cooked a turkey before, right? I asked.

It'll work out, he said. And with that, out Larry went to invite the Lynchburg-lonely to Thanksgiving dinner at our tiny duplex apartment on Euclid Ave., all 600 square feet of it.

The day before Thanksgiving I asked him if he knew how many people might be coming the next day. There's no way to know, he said.

How will I know how much food to prepare, and how will we pay for it? I asked again, throwing my eyes toward our pitiful, newlywed checkbook.

I told people to bring whatever they could, that we will provide the turkey and dressing, he said. There will be plenty of turkey.

OK, I said. Hmmm.

We woke on our first frosty Virginia Thanksgiving morning. Larry had to work the seven-to-three shift at the gas company, so I spent the morning home alone with the turkey. Making the dressing was a snap. My mother's cornbread dressing is the best there is, and she had given me the clear and detailed instructions passed down to her from her mother and *her* mother. (For the record, for Southern folk, proper cornbread dressing is a big deal, a very big deal.)

As far as the turkey goes, that was another story. While there are many theories on turkey-roasting best practices, my parents always roasted their turkeys in a browning bag, claiming this the best method. Mother had given me instructions for this as well. I was to stuff the turkey's tail-end full of onions and apples and celery for flavor, but before that, I was to slather butter all over the outside of the bird, lift and place him into the browning bag, and then cram his tail-end full of fruits and vegetables.

For company, I turned the Thanksgiving Day Parade on in the little den and grabbed the butter plate. Thanksgiving dinner, *tsk,* a piece of cake, I thought with the arrogance only a naïve, untested, proud beginner who never cooked a turkey before can honestly believe.

First of all, this turkey was a little stubborn, refusing to part from his packaging with ease, the wrapping getting hung up rather grandly on his hind quarters and feet for a few tense minutes (wait, does this turkey have feet?), but nothing unmanageable. I wished for a minute Larry was there to help me, a couple of extra hands never hurt anyone, especially me – remember the little three-fingered affair on my left hand – so my fully-functioning right hand can sometimes use a little help around the kitchen with projects that require lifting and grabbing.

But I'm no weakling; I'm bigger than this turkey and I've certainly faced more formidable foes. Packaging be damned.

Next, get this bad-boy buttered-up.

The turkey sat on the counter top, the maw of the browning bag opened wide, ready for the turkey's grand entrance. I had remembered to set the butter out to soften, so I took a mighty handful and slapped the turkey confidently on the back and began to slather him with gusto, starting at his front end and gliding toward his rear with relative speed.

In every good story there is the hour of great tension and empirical angst, the point of no return. One last cry of protest shouted to the universe before succumbing to the inevitable over which one has no control. Little did I know, but this was the turkey's moment, his existential revolt, his last stand. Shout he could not, but squirm he could.

As my buttery hands reached the turkey's impressive shanks, I must have grasped his legs overly hard with my eight oily digits, for he began to move, yes, he started sliding down the short runway of the cheap Formica countertop heading headlong toward the dark abyss that was my unswept linoleum floor. The more I grabbed at him in panic, the more momentum he gained. I ran to the end of the counter with my butter-hands held chest high, trying to head him off at the pass, but alas, my attempts proved futile. That turkey sailed with remarkable poise and speed right off the countertop and landed rather elegantly onto the dog's bowl, kibbles and water creating a glorious sort of *splashdown* effect as he landed and slid just a bit more, finally resting at the threshold of our small den amid soft cheers from the folk at the Macy's Thanksgiving Day Parade.

Our little dog Brandy began to lick great globs of butter from the floor.

Well. This Thanksgiving dinner might *literally* be a piece of cake.

If the Internet had existed then, I could have Googled *How to get a buttery twenty-five-pound turkey off the floor with only one hand.*

But there was no Internet back in the olden days, so I was left to my own devices and this situation: I didn't know who or even how many people would be coming for dinner, and I didn't know for sure if any of them would bring any food. Since the potential existed that turkey and dressing might be the only fare for this meal, I had to get this turkey off the floor and into the oven, and pronto.

I quick-assessed the damage. The turkey lay languid on the floor, tail-end up and open.

Have you ever looked up a large turkey's tail-end? It's big, cavernous in fact, with plenty of room to stuff things like apples and onions and celery. Or a fist. When there's nothing left to do, one does what one must. I made a firm fist with my strong right hand and stuffed it hard up that turkey's butt, lifting him upward with all my strength. Surely lifting a big, buttery, twenty-five-pound turkey the long four feet from the floor to the countertop with only one arm crammed up his butt constitutes a true Herculean feat. I challenge all you gym-folk to give it a go, if you dare.

The turkey required a hefty cleaning before he made it to his final resting place; no one likes a crunchy turkey. Pick, pick, pick – after removing, nay, extracting from the turkey's buttery back and behind an undetermined number of dog food kibbles, way too much floor fuzz, and a Cheerio or two, the fowl was presentable enough to try again. Slowly into the browning bag I shoved him, both of us exhausted from our epic struggle.

Woman versus beast has never had more meaning.

Sometime in the midst of it all, Larry telephoned. How's it going? he asked.

Great, I said. Turkey's in the oven, all's right with the world.

Fourteen people showed up late that afternoon, none of whom we knew. Two college guys came to the door with one bag of Doritos and a pint of onion dip. One girl brought a Coke – one Coke. The motorcycle-gang guy from across the street came and brought his girlfriend and a loaf of day-old bread from the Wonder thrift store down the block. A store-bought pumpkin pie appeared from thin air. The rest of the folk had no food to add to the celebration. They probably just forgot.

So, we sixteen pilgrims sat on the wooden floor and the few chairs of our tiny Lynchburg duplex with paper plates full and gave thanks. We ate turkey and dressing, Doritos and onion dip. I had plenty of butter for the day-old bread, and we even had dessert. Turns out, one pumpkin pie can indeed feed sixteen mouths, for little becomes much when it is blessed with thanksgiving.

I found a kibble in a bite of my turkey. I feel quite sure that others did as well, but no one said anything.

Except *thank you.*

I Am Switzerland

I am Switzerland.

I stay away from conflict and avoid taking sides. Neutral I am and neutral I shall remain.

It's pretty here and the snow is pristine and untouched, and I could live here forever.

Until I can no more.

I am a peace negotiator.

I could have worked for the UN and spoken thirteen languages and negotiated peace treaties around the globe and been famous for it like Madeline Albright and Henry Kissinger.

I could have performed that job well with my natural sanguine personality, happy when everyone at the table is happy, even when the conflicts are raw or unsettled or cheaply masked, as long as we are all smiling for the picture.

Until I could no more.

I am the one in the family who makes everybody laugh.

Like that time my father had surgery for colon cancer, and I brought the balloons and the food and made all the jokes about colons while my brother blew up a latex glove and made a turkey out of the glove and I gave the turkey a face with Sharpies from the bottom of my purse.

I'm the one who took the picture of us all smiling and posted it on social media after the surgery was successful.

Until I was no more.

I am a peacemaker.

Blessed are my kind, right?, for we shall be called the children of God.

I have always been happy and content with my God-given ability as peacemaker.

I am quite good at it, so I've always thought, and if I had gotten a tattoo ten years ago it might have read *Peace, Be Still* emblazoned across the wings of a snow-white dove but what I would have meant was *Peace At All Costs.*

Until my good friend finally asked me, Are you a peacemaker, or a peacekeeper?

They are not the same thing, she said.

And this realization was hard for me, for I knew she was right.

Turns out, I was not a peacemaker but rather a peacekeeper.

Until I was not.

When my other friend's child bullied the Black child in his class and my friend didn't want to do anything about it and they did not invite the Black child to the birthday party, my nature shouted to me, Look away, it's not your problem, it's not your kid doing the bullying.

But I spoke and my friend did not appreciate my butting into her business and we now act like friends but know we are not any longer.

These things are hard for me.

I hate conflict and I love peace.

I brag about being an Enneagram 9 until I finally realize I am not.

I love peace, that's partly why I believe in Heaven.

But until then I will keep trying my hand at peace-*making* in this tiny corner of the universe that is mine.

Even though it is very hard for me.

A Letter to my Students, Nov 2016

Friday morning, November 4, 2016.

A mere four days before the Presidential election of 2016 and a heap of poetry analysis papers has set up a campsite on my desk, at the ready, begging with each passing hour to be read. I'm trying to decide whether to cart the pile home with me for the weekend or let them settle in on my desk until Monday.

We are all exhausted. It's the end of what's been an excruciating election season – our entire nation feels it, united are we but in an odd, hard-to-name distemper. We are tired of the talking and tired of listening to the worst episode of He said/She said in modern history. My senior girls are worried and sad, wishing they could be a bit more optimistic and excited about voting in their very first Presidential election.

Wondering what the world will look like on Wednesday.

At the moment, it is quiet here in my classroom, room 374. I look up from grading. Girls are in here studying, working out their ideas and figuring out the best ways to express them on paper.

Scholars are these, girls who think.

Today, three girls sit together on my couch hunched quiet over computers, writing. One writes on the objectification of women in *Othello*, another scribbles notes on the crippling nature of indecision in *Hamlet,* and the third examines how T.S. Eliot's late-in-life religious conversion affects the tone and message of his poetry. Scholars are these, girls who think; and for people who think, this particular election cycle has thrown us all for a loop.

My AP classes are reading Dostoevsky's *Crime and Punishment* at this time in history. We are at the point in the novel where the murderer Raskolnikov, in a fitful state of mind, returns to the scene of the crime to admire his own bloody workmanship, only to find the apartment where he murdered the old crone and her sister freshly painted over, whitewashed. Astounded and angry that his grisly handiwork has been cleaned up, Raskolnikov screams with fury at the painter, Where's the blood, what happened to the blood? The lone painter shakes his head dumbfounded and steps back to examine this man Raskolnikov, to take a good long look at the person who dares such a return, and with demands to boot! What arrogance! The painter then whispers his own astonished question: *What sort of man are you?*

My students, young women I love so much, this is indeed the question of this day. Not who are you or who do you want to be, but rather Dostoevsky's subtle variation of this question.

What *sort* of person are you? What *sort* of person are you becoming?

Before I dare to ask you to consider this question, though, I feel the need to apologize on behalf of the many adults in your lives who have failed you, failed to give you worthy role models, failed to be honest. Shakespeare's Falstaff understands when he says, *Lord, Lord, how subject we old men are to this vice of lying … every third word a lie…* Indeed. World leaders and musicians and politicians and CEOs and professional athletes and entertainers and the media and influencers and sometimes teachers and sometimes parents. People who may or may not have asked themselves this question, *What sort of person am I?* We the grown-ups, in embarrassingly large numbers, have not been examples of goodness for you.

One thing I admire about you young women is that you don't tolerate much nonsense, and we have certainly thrown a great deal of nonsense your way. Add the fact that so many of us spend so many of our waking hours with our noses stuck in screens, we can become drenched in the muck of disappointment, and it seems easier than ever to lose sight of goodness and the hope for better.

With that caveat acknowledged, I ask you this. Do you think you could ever set aside your mentality toward blame – which we your elders sadly bequeathed to you, again, I'm so sorry – for one quick second and ask yourself to think honestly and vulnerably?

If you can, then ask yourself this question. Go ahead and say it out loud, no one is listening. No one is here but you.

What sort of person am I?

Try as hard as you can to resist asking *this* question: Yeah, but what about everybody else? What sort of people are Hillary and Donald and Anthony Weiner and Mr. Hyde and Lord Voldemort and Captain Ahab and Hannibal Lector and Iago and Cain and Beelzebub and Nurse Ratched and the Wicked Witch of the West? What about them, huh? What sort of people are they?

I do not know. Dear students-of-mine, you know this isn't new, don't you? The list of ne'er-do-wells stretches from the dawn of time to the edges of eternity. Always has, always will. I'm not talking about them. I don't know them and don't want to. I'm talking about you. It is you I love, it is your character and happiness that compels me to ask you to consider what *sort* of person you are.

And while we're searching our innards, let's not forget about goodness, even if we don't see enough of it these days. And patience and kindness and generosity and faithfulness and gentleness and self-control, and above all love, which does not envy or boast, does not dishonor others and is not proud or self-seeking, is not easily angered. Love, which protects and trusts and hopes and always perseveres.

Are we people who love, is that the *sort* of people we are?

What is your plan for Wednesday if your candidate does not win? Do you know what you will say or do or not do, have you thought about the day after? The answer to this question is indicative of your character and who you are as a human being.

You may have to do the role modeling, my dear ones. It may be the children who lead us toward civility – you might remember that's what the Book says, *A little child will lead us.* That's you.

So, Tuesday we vote and Wednesday we have answers. Do not look for good role modeling on the news on Wednesday morning for I fear you will not find it there. Wednesday's news cycle will be filled with all sorts of individuals acting as they will act, saying what they will say, judging as they will judge.

But as I said earlier, I don't know them, I know you. It is your peace and your character and your good life I care about. So let us gather together and fight the good fight right where we are. Someone needs to do it, someone must start.

For me, it happens in room 374. Chin up. I'll see you there tomorrow.

Geezer

His grandchildren called him Geezer. In fact, in the days immediately after the birth of his first grandchild, everyone called my father Geezer, his self-chosen grandfather name. It was such an awesome grandpa-name that we always forgot it sounded disrespectful when shouted in public by our entire family of loud-talkers. Little six-year-old kids shouting, Hey Geezer, come look at this! down church hallways and in restaurants and department stores, has brought us decades of scornful glances and pursed lips from crabby little old ladies and members of sophisticated wait staffs.

But if you knew my father at all, you called him Geezer, too.

In 2011, Geezer was diagnosed with Parkinson's. We sat together in their quiet den and Nanny spoke the word. In families, each person has his particular role, or at least that's how it is in our family. Nanny is my nurse-mother, the strength in the worst of times. Geezer and I are the criers. Husband Larry is quiet, he prays a lot. After the word *Parkinson's* entered the room and the tears fell, we set about understanding the business of this new road untraveled. Neurologists, medications. My mother busy online reading reading reading about symptoms and side effects. Coconut oil, vitamin E, physical exercise, keep moving, keep moving.

Geezer was a Sunday School teacher his entire adult life. He taught junior high kids in the youth room of Whitehaven Presbyterian Church, young adults and young married couples at Broadway Baptist. If you live in Memphis or ever did, he's probably taught you or someone you know in Sunday School somewhere along the way. It *is* the South, for Heaven's sake and God bless us, we love us some Sunday School.

Geezer got up early every morning of his life to read and study for his Sunday School lesson. *Every* morning. Commentaries and strong coffee in hand, seated in the serenity of his booky den, Geezer sacrificed several hours of sleep each day to the discipline of study and reflection. This is one of my earliest memories of my father and the most important.

My husband Larry observed this morning ritual when he was a young man courting Geezer's daughter and saw a fine example of how to be a godly man by watching how a godly man goes about his day. Larry chose to live his life in the same fashion, rising early every day to sit in a book-filled room to study and pray, strong coffee and legal pad in hand.

My son-in-law Coleton now does the same thing. He too watched this morning ritual when he was a young man courting Larry's daughter and saw an example of how to be a god-fearing man by watching how god-fearing men start their day. Now he rises early every morning to study and pray, strong coffee in hand and an iPad filled with commentaries.

It's the blessing, what we pass down to our children and our children's children. Blessings or curses, it seems we have some choice.

Geezer had been teaching the same adult Sunday School class for over twenty-five years, a large class, 150 strong, many of whom became friends – real friends, I mean – and now were growing old together. The lovely, fragile gift of companions, mates, sojourners walking similar paths at similar times.

For everything there is a season and a time for every purpose under heaven. The time came for Geezer to tell his Sunday School class about his diagnosis. Time to speak the word in public, time to be courageous.

I called Geezer and asked, Would you like for me to come and sit with you and Nanny on Sunday when you tell the class about your Parkinson's?

Yes, I would.

So that's what I did.

It was a regular Southern Baptist Sunday School kind of day. Warm Memphis sun outside, requisite coffee and doughnuts inside. Dresses and panty hose and heels and dark suits with bright ties. Noisy, loud, church conversation interrupted only by the raucous and cacophonous cackle from bevies of lip-sticked magnolias. Seriously, women in the South know how to laugh.

My presence in the room was the only thing out of the ordinary on that most ordinary Sunday, and even with that, I am not an unknown entity to this group, my parents' lovely gaggle of friends who have given so many bridal and baby showers and birthday parties and receptions for all of us that we could never begin to repay.

Geezer taught his lesson well that day, although for the life of me I cannot recall what he taught on. My mother says she can't either. We sat dutifully on the front row; the lesson was not the foremost thought on our minds. Geezer was going to tell them of his diagnosis, this is what we waited for. The lesson was over, the time had come.

I'm not sure, but I think my mother dreaded this moment the most. A spoken word cannot be retracted. *What's done cannot be undone*, Shakespeare's Macbeth said, and of course, he's right. Like gossip and slander and porno-photographs on the Internet, once it's out there, it's out there. It cannot be undone or taken back. Geezer will tell his story and everyone will know he has Parkinson's and then it will be real.

Some had suspected this; a few of their closest friends had been hinting to my mother that something seemed amiss – true friends do that sort of thing. Geezer had had a good bit of trouble saying the prayer at my daughter's wedding.

Geezer closed his Bible and spoke his piece. I know that many of you have wondered what's been going on with me lately health-wise. Well, like my mother before me, I have been diagnosed with Parkinson's.

I heard the proverbial pin drop. For a moment or two, we all settled into the word he said, the word all of us heard but none of us wanted. But Geezer-the-Brave was not finished with his proclamation, his declaration, his moment. Not yet. He stood with his back unusually straight.

Now remember I said that Geezer and I are the criers and my mother is the nurse-mother who is the strength most of the time. Well, this bright hot summer Sunday irony was at play and my parents switched roles. My mother started fishing Kleenex out of her enormous bag-of-bags like they were trout in an Alaskan stream and her friends did the same and they all passed them around amidst great waves of sniffing and snorting.

For Geezer, though, the moment was different. This was his time, and in it he was fearless, tearless, and I too was unusually tearless, stoic even, watching my hero stand high before his troops on their parade ground and tell them all that he, too, was human and subject to the weaknesses and ills that age and time bring. That he, like Hamlet, must consider *the heart-ache and the thousand natural shocks that flesh is heir to.*

No one is exempt. Geezer-the-Fearless spoke the real word aloud and it had not destroyed him; in fact, he seemed to gain momentum in this moment, a strength unexpected. He continued to speak with his Bible his sword his long-time companion in hand.

Job said it best, my father said. He was smitten with all sorts of troubles – boils and bankruptcy and death of family and a negative, critical wife and the worst friends ever. Yet he looked it all in the face, his own loss and destruction *and* his God, and he managed to spit out the words:

What? shall we receive good at the hand of God and not receive evil?

Both the profundity and the simplicity of the question overwhelmed me. Snippets of my own recent struggle with hardship flooded over me, along with the struggles of history, millennia past, a lifetime of stories about adversities encountered by saints and heroes flash into memory as my Geezer stood before us. I thought of my favorite hymn which was composed by Lesbia Scott for her children in the 1920's and sung in chapel at St. Mary's, my school, on All-Saint's Day.

I sing a song of the saints of God, patient and brave and true,
Who toiled and fought and lived and died for the Lord they loved and knew.
And one was a doctor, and one was a queen, and one was shepherdess on the green,
They were all of them saints of God, and I mean, God helping, to be one too.

On that bright Sunday morn, Geezer joined the saints of the song who toiled and fought and lived and died through good and bad and ease and difficulty and profit and loss, it all comes from the same hand, a good Hand that through the years Geezer and the other saints have taught me to trust.

Watching him I understood how the truth can set us free, for my brave father stood there dripping in the stuff of freedom.

The small miracle took place after the benediction and the last Amen of the morning. I heard rustlings behind me and turned eager to see an impromptu geezer-line forming, a battalion 150 strong, fists stuffed with clumps of damp Kleenex, with encouragement on their lips and in their eyes. These comrades-in-arms who were facing the same struggles in their lives, who understood experientially as well as existentially that, as Thornton Wilder wisely put it, this is the way it is in our growing up and in our marrying and in our living and in our dying.

I did not know all their names, but this day was no day for names; this day was about walking alongside the best they could with their crutches and walkers and oxygen tanks and prostheses and hearing aids and trifocals and a wheelchair or two or three, this line of fellow countrymen, citizens of the same point in time, formed to comfort my father – their leader – to bless him and join hands and hearts on this road all feet will trod.

They know one of the great secrets that some never know, that walking together means not having to walk alone.

Geezer loved to fish at Pickwick Lake, and he'd fished with Jerry and Don and Bob and David for a long long time; the fish stories among this crew are as countless as the stars, some actually true.

This day the fishermen were serious, though, and standing beside Geezer when the anglers made their way to the front of the line, I overheard their quiet talk at Geezer's side, their fish tales this day honest and vulnerable.

Don took Geezer's already shaky hand. I'm not ready to give up fishing, Geezer admitted, his voice breaking for the first time, so I guess I'm just going to fish until I can't bait the hook anymore.

Don, the spokesman for the fisherman quartet, put it very simply. Don't worry, Geezer. When that happens, we'll be right alongside to bait the hook for you.

I sing a song of the saints of God, patient and brave and true.

Lord Tennyson's poem "Ulysses" recounts the aging of the great Greek hero of the same name and states the sentiment more eloquently than any other. Ulysses speaks of the companions who accompanied him on his adventures throughout his lifetime of struggles, through both the thunder and the sunshine, when he says,

> *Tho' much is taken, much abides; and tho'*
> *We are not now that strength which in old days*
> *Moved earth and heaven; that which we are, we are;*
> *One equal temper of heroic hearts,*
> *Made weak by time and fate, but strong in will*
> *To strive, to seek, to find, and not to yield.*

So don't yield, Saint Geezer. Keep striving, seeking, finding, and not yielding. The other saints, past and present, what your precious Book calls *the great cloud of witnesses*, are flanking you, holding you up with good words, and song.

They were all of them saints of God, and I mean, God helping, to be one too.

And I mean it, God help me to be one too.

W. B. Yeats (1865-1939)

The Second Coming

Turning and turning in the widening gyre
The falcon cannot hear the falconer;
Things fall apart; the centre cannot hold;
Mere anarchy is loosed upon the world,
The blood-dimmed tide is loosed, and everywhere
The ceremony of innocence is drowned;
The best lack all conviction, while the worst
Are full of passionate intensity.
Surely some revelation is at hand;
Surely the Second Coming is at hand.
The Second Coming! Hardly are those words out
When a vast image out of Spiritus Mundi
Troubles my sight: somewhere in sands of the desert
A shape with lion body and the head of a man,
A gaze blank and pitiless as the sun,
Is moving its slow thighs, while all about it
Reel shadows of the indignant desert birds.
The darkness drops again; but now I know
That twenty centuries of stony sleep
Were vexed to nightmare by a rocking cradle,
And what rough beast, its hour come round at last,
Slouches towards Bethlehem to be born?

So, What Do I Do Now?

Have you read "The Second Coming" by W.B. Yeats since high school, or college, or ever? I love to teach this poem because Yeats gets right to the point with his terse, unapologetic concision, *Things fall apart; the center cannot hold.* My goodness but he's bleak.

But if you've been around here more than a minute or two, you know what he's talking about. If you've watched a movie or read a novel or lost a relationship or had a good conversation or listened to a podcast, then you've seen it, breathed it, felt it settle deep into your lungs and bones – the bentness of things on this lovely planet of ours, this odd, often ironic, bent quality of being, the center of which cannot hold.

Once we've tasted the acrid piquancy of brokenness, long-lingering on the tongue like a bitter pill or an accidental bite of chalk, we wince ever in remembrance.

Once we've felt our losses deep as the sea and endless as the desert, we shake our heads in agreement with the poet.

Once we've lived through a long-lingering pandemic, we know

Yeats tells the truth. Things fall apart and will do so again, and if we live long enough, then yet again.

So, what does one do when things don't go the way one expects or wants or needs or feels entitled to, and while we are at it, what happens when *my* things fall apart? More than once I have tried stamping my foot and arching my shoulders back and throwing my voice Heavenward, but I am always left wondering if anyone is listening.

I have shouted What do I do now? How shall I live? but so far, my frantic tantrums and the buckets of my hot tears have not yet straightened out the bent, not one little bit. It's as crooked as it's been since the serpent winked at Eve and whispered the best lie of all, the doozy to end all doozies, the grand-pappy of all lies, the one so strong it tilted this old world on its axis.

Surely, thou shalt not die. Not you, Eve, not you.

In the novel *Tess of the d'Urbervilles,* Tess Durbeyfield declares in fatalistic surety that we have landed on "a blighted star," and she's certainly not the first to think it. History startles me every time, especially when I forget to remember that I must ponder yesterday before I can fully consider today.

Yesterday an election was lost and won.

Yesterday somewhere between 50 and 80 million people died in a second world war.

Yesterday a brother slew his brother and then hid from God, leaving Him asking, Cain, where is your brother?

Yesterday a mother would not forgive her husband and so he moved away from his own children to another city and began a new life.

Yesterday the Challenger exploded.

Yesterday 15,891 people died in a tsunami in Japan.

Yesterday six parents died in an airplane accident, leaving eleven children behind.

Yesterday another teenage girl was sold into sex trafficking.

Yesterday a baby girl was born with a deformed arm and hand.

Yesterday a baby boy was born with a cleft palette.

Yesterday a mother died after losing a hard bout with cancer, and two men I loved died in the same month from Parkinson's with dementia.

Yesterday two airplanes flew into two tall towers.

Things fall apart. It's true, the center cannot hold.

So, what in the world are we supposed to do now? What in heck is going on here?

God knows, but He doesn't seem to tell us.

We need some help. But, who? Who among us shall ascend to the hill of the Lord? Who shall stand in his holy place? Who among us shall ascend, whom shall we send?

I search the Internet but find no takers, no one suitable, no not one. There is no one to send, no one to save us, not a single hand or heart clean enough, not one body courageous enough, not one innocent enough – we are too blasted busy. We think yesterday was somehow more wholesome and honest, easier, and certainly crammed with fewer activities. We seek our saviors in voting booths and then riot afterward in the online streets, realizing (yet again) that these are women and men who live among us, not gods, and we are still surprised every single time and have been since the first dawn.

We think our hour is unique in time and space. And so it is and so it isn't. It's simply our turn, our day, nothing more. There will never be another day like this one.

Until tomorrow.

Whom shall we send? Who among us shall ascend?

Yesterday Abraham was the chosen one but in human moments of raw fear and weakness, he lied, calling Sarah his sister and giving her to a neighboring king.

Yesterday Moses was chosen but wasn't it he who came down from the mountain and smashed the tablets in anger, he who literally broke God's word into dust to blow away into the hot desert sands and to the ends of the earth?

Yesterday David was chosen but it turns out even giant-killers are mere mortals with hearts grand for God and wills thin and fragile as webs.

Abraham Lincoln was the man chosen for his time but I read he was known for sacrificing principles in the name of expediency. Should I believe everything I read?

In a letter estimated to be from 1961, Mother Teresa of Calcutta wrote: *Darkness is such that I really do not see – neither with my mind nor with my reason – the place of God in my soul is blank – There is no God in me* – Great, even Mother Teresa.

So, in my weakness I shout again, What is happening and is there Anyone paying attention?

To be human is to become accustomed to the sour after-smack of pain and fear lying on my palate, yesterday and tomorrow. To know the slap of disappointment – especially of self – and to bear its subtle sting on the cheek like post-op numbness. To remember the bentness of things and people. To acknowledge that Life is curvy, and bent.

But wait, that cannot be the whole of it. Turns out, the sum is greater than its parts after all; could this be the beginning of the definition of hope? If so, whom do we hope to send? Alas. There is no one but us, and no time but now. Bent us, crooked now.

What an odd system.

Yeats' poem concludes with this terrifying question, apocalyptic in tone, its breadth of scope enormous and eerily ever-relevant: *And what rough beast, its hour come round at last, / Slouches towards Bethlehem to be born?* Yeats asks the question on everyone's lips, then and now, whether we are paying attention or not: Who is next, what is next? What rough beast will rise up next, heading even now toward his own town and time to be born?

But I say, that is not the whole of it, for the poets also seem to ask, *Ah, but a man's reach should exceed his grasp, / Or what's a Heaven for?*

If I change one small word in Yeats' question, I have an entirely different question. One word indeed makes all the difference.

Perhaps that's why Christ's metaphor for Himself was the Word.

If I replace the word *rough* with *benevolent*, the poem is hopeful.

If I replace the word *rough* with *kind*, the poem is confident.

If I replace the word *rough* with *loving*, the poem saves me. The hour has come at last!

What a difference one word makes. So, for Heaven's sake, replace the word!

Is it as easy as that? Can I pick up kindness and grace and humility and goodness and be born and reborn like the sun, new every single morning? Can I really choose to put these new clothes on like a mantle, re-clothe myself in this character? Am I allowed these sartorial choices even here on this messy planet in my wild and lovely, totally bent life?

Yes and yes and yes and yes. Like salve on a wound, like oil on the head, like fragrance on spring's first bloom, like the smell of a wood fire on autumn's first cold night, there is indeed a balm in Gilead. Who shall ascend? Who can make a difference, small or otherwise?

ME, bent and broken me.

YOU, crooked and splintered you.

Gerard Manley Hopkins reminds me of this, oh how I love his wonderfully enigmatic poetic style:

And for all this, nature is never spent;
There lives the dearest freshness deep down things;
And though the last lights off the black West went
Oh, morning, at the brown brink eastward, springs
Because the Holy Ghost over the bent
World broods with warm breast and with ah! bright wings.

So, what do I do now? Get up, put on my new clothes, and get to work. Kindness takes a lot of energy and a good part of my day. I may slouch a bit, but I will pick up my crutch and hobble toward Bethlehem to be born.

WINTER

My Terribly Beautiful Corner

My Nissan Rogue has the road memorized, it's automatic now. I choose the music or the silence, and the car makes its way to Kirby Pines Lifecare Community – left onto Poplar, right onto Estate, left on Quince, right on Kirby. It's an easy drive, taking all things into consideration.

My mother's text read, Could you please come today, just for an hour? She greets me at her door. Her eyes are tired and red, and her wrinkles seem a bit more pronounced every time I see her. Her friends say she's holding up well, but I wonder. I'll watch my father for an hour or two while my mother goes to the store. Or maybe she'll just drive around or take a walk or cry in the parking lot like I found her that first morning after she bravely dropped Geezer off at Dementia Day Care. All will be well, I texted her that morning. We'll see, she replied.

A wise older friend of mine once said this about the aches of aging: if you live long enough, everybody gets a turn. The same is true for tending to aging parents. It's like an ironic return to childhood with diapers and droppers of medicine and tears and tantrums and sleep all day and stay up all night. That 2:00 am phone call from my mother that Geezer had gone missing, out the front door and down the stairs in his pajamas – literally with one shoe off and one shoe on like Deedle Deedle Dumpling. Can you and Larry please come and help me find him?

The parent becoming the child takes some getting used to on everyone's part.

How do? my father says when I sit in the recliner next to him, my memories of him filled with this little phrase *How do?* I'm great, how are you?

Fox News blares with impeachment and Pelosi and a trade deal with Canada and I am weary beyond description of this boulder of futility. I turn the volume on the television down, way down, and look at my father. I think he knows me. He looks and sounds clear.

How are you doing? I ask.

I'm pooped, he says. Your mother had me up in the trees all day yesterday, chain-sawing and cutting back branches, mowing the yard. My arms are aching.

Yesterday was Dementia Day Care day.

She's got you working hard, I say.

Yes, but she knows how I love working in the yard.

He always did.

After a while he stands up to wander around the house, take a little inventory. Their house is loaded with the antiques they collected over sixty-two years together and he stops to admire each plate, each clock, each lamp, seeing the old as new, one selfsame thing new again every morning. He touches a blue-and-white Majolica pitcher shaped like a jumping fish with a gaping mouth, the one bought in Antwerp in that antique shop he loved so, on the tiny side street close to our house. Now, isn't this purty? he says, quite sure he's never seen this pitcher before. It is, I say. He notices a painting of old Bruges and her many bridges housed in an ornate, heavy golden frame, the one he bought in Van Elsen's shop in the Philipstockstraat, the shop by the belfry. Now, that's mighty purty, isn't it? he remarks. I wonder what that's a picture of. That's in Belgium, I say. A beautiful city called Bruges. I'd like to go there one day, he says. OK, let's go, I say and he smiles in agreement.

Off he shuffles toward the bedroom. I worry he'll slip and fall so I hand him his cane which he dutifully holds but refuses to employ. When we insist, he'll carry the cane, but he hooks the curve of the walking stick over on his arm like the Queen of England carrying her purse. My family can't decide if he has forgotten how to place the cane on the ground for balance or if he's reminding us once-and-for-all, with stolid reserve, You might can make me *hold* the cane but you cannot make me *use* the cane – I think I see a defiant, last existential protest in his mischievous eyes.

It is when he looks up on the bedroom wall and sees our family portrait in its gold frame that this moment is forced to its crisis. In this portrait, our entire family is seated in wicker chairs on my parents' back porch, the children still young then, everyone still young, everyone smiling. But this morning in a sliver of clarity, a blink of an eye, a thin opening back into memory for a single instant, Geezer sees the portrait, he *really* sees it and remembers all the players and the lovely day and the children small and the joy and the white clothing and the light spring breeze and the soft gurgle of the water flowing from the fountain, and recognition of these moments ripple across his face in an odd wave of memory, remembrance tossed with floods of joy and convoluted with the agony of pain and mixed with memory lost, as if all of his craniofacial muscles understood at once and flexed and strained in a unique joining of the difficult present and the lovely past in one, in a brief, fleeting moment of beautiful recollection.

The veil lifted. He remembers those people in the photograph, each one of them, and the painful beauty of what was now marries the reality of what is, and it is too terribly beautiful and Geezer begins to weep. His words escape him, Parkinson's stole them some time back, his eyes speak for him now. I don't know how to fix this – there's no fixing this! – so I say the first things I can think of, which this time, thankfully, are the truth.

You made this happen, I whisper, the beauty in this photograph, you and Nanny made this. This is your doing, you know. All these people, these are your people and everyone in this picture loves you beyond measure, remember?

His weepy eyes asked me if everyone in the photo was doing well. Yes, I say, we are all well, everybody is good and happy and educated and have jobs and no one is hungry and most everybody is married now with children of their own and we take care of each other. No need to worry about a thing.

And as quickly as it came, it departed. The thick veil returned and the family in the photo withdrew back into the distant past and the old man's tears dried and we went back to sit in the faded recliners and Geezer fell immediately asleep; he's had a big day, a big emotional day. I sit beside him and hold his hand.

The second law of thermodynamics demands that the total entropy of a system either increases or remains constant, it never decreases. Entropy is a zero in a reversible process, it increases in an irreversible process. Things grow smaller thinner weaker feebler more fragile as they age and decline, so turns this world of ours. And yet, the smaller my corner of the universe gets, the happier I become, it seems. I don't know why this situation has surprised me, but it has. There is a time for everything, a time for every purpose under Heaven, and this is my time to take care of those who took care of me. So, I sit with my father to give my mother a moment to herself; I heat up his soup, bring those chocolate cookies he likes, help him to the restroom, tell him all the stories over again, and wipe his tears.

And my tiny corner of the universe, on this day during this difficult time in my life, is filled with delight unmeasured.

The winter solstice for the Northern Hemisphere
The shortest day, the longest night

Winter Solstice

On this day, at a mathematically precise point in time – 7:59 am in the year of our Lord 2021 – the northernmost point of the Earth will tilt farther from the sun, farther from the light, than any other day of the year. The winter solstice for the Northern Hemisphere. The shortest day, the longest night.

Today the weakened sun's rays will illuminate the icy streets of Helsinki for less than six hours, a remarkable thirteen hours and a handful of minutes fewer than these same Helsinkians will enjoy at the summer solstice in June.

And the citizenry of Utqiagvik, which sits a cozy 320 miles north of the Arctic Circle and 515 miles south of the North Pole, will sit and walk and read and play and shop and hunt and prepare dinner for their families in the semi-darkness all this livelong day, for the sun hides at the edges of their Alaskan horizon on this, the shortest of all our days, and refuses to leave his hiding place for up to two months.

We dwell in a land of extremes. Great moments of light and darkness remind us that Nature reveals as well as conceals, as does her Maker, and not to acknowledge both is not to believe our own eyes.

Winter's morning bird must work for her breakfast crumbs

for they lie hidden beneath the winter's cold snow, yet nonetheless the steadfast wren sings her morning song with courageous abandon. Go outside and listen, can you hear her? I listen now as she sings: *No matter how long the night lasts, the morning is sure to come.*

The poet Thomas Hardy (1840-1928) writes of a such a bird, an old, darkling thrush who dares to sing of joy in the dark! What courage!

At once a voice arose among
The bleak twigs overhead,
In a full-hearted evensong
Of joy illimited.
An aged thrush, frail, gaunt and small,
With blast-beruffled plume,
Had chosen thus to fling his soul
Upon the growing gloom…

Do I dare sing in the dark? What might happen if I, like an aging bird, flung my soul upon the growing gloom?

The angels sang *Glory to God in the Highest* in the darkest of dark night to a clutch of poor working-class men, a bedraggled bunch of shepherds, and those guys had the gumption to listen in the darkness and flee their flocks and jump headlong into the unknown realms of pure faith. And the rest is miracle.

Perhaps miracles happen most often in the darkness; maybe in the brightness of day, we think we need no such thing.

It is rare to find folk who achieve great things without first spending some time in the dark.

It is true that the fine folk of Utqiagvik will go a couple of months without seeing the sun, but this they know: the sun returns, and come May, the "midnight sun" will bring months and months and months of warm light, as long as this old world continues to spin.

Tomorrow the days will begin again to lengthen, the earth will start to lean back toward the light. Nature brings us to brightness only through the dark – there is no other way. For if there is light, there must also be shadows.

Amos 5:8 – *Seek him that maketh the seven stars and Orion, and turneth the shadow of death into the morning, and maketh the day dark with night: that calleth for the waters of the sea and poureth them out upon the face of the earth: The LORD is his name.*

Rock Tumblers

My brother Eric had a rock tumbler as a kid, and in the early 1970s, a rock tumbler was a mighty fine apparatus to have in one's garage since rocks were, as they always have been, fairly easy to come by.

In those days, smooth, tumbled stones were the fashion rage in bracelets and necklaces, right alongside puka shell necklaces and bellbottom jeans. Rather than flying to exotic places like Hawaii or Tahiti, the Brand family instead pulled a camper-trailer on vacation, thus finding any puka shells became a glorious pipe dream that lay far outside the realm of any family jewelry-making enterprises.

And our bellbottoms came from Sears, though we were loathe to tell anybody.

So, my brother tumbled rocks and made necklaces for our mother, and, if I remember correctly, was feelin' quite groovy.

This tumbled-stone necklace is so unique, I'll wear this to the PTA meeting, cooed my mother. That's hippy jewelry, my father mumbled. Damn hippies. (The only time I ever heard my father curse was in front of the word "hippies.")

Since we grew up camping, my brother found rocks everywhere we went, stones from the Little River in the Great Smoky Mountains and the Buffalo River in Arkansas, collecting and hauling home rocks large-and-small to see what would happen to them in the tumbler.

Do you remember Lucille Ball in that movie *The Long Long Trailer* where she collects rocks everywhere she stops on her honeymoon camping trip and the camper nearly tumbles over the side of the Sierra Nevada Mountains?

That was us. My father pulled our Shasta trailer up and down the Smoky ranges of Tennessee and the Ozarks of Arkansas, and one time all the way to Carlsbad Caverns, and Eric picked up rocks rocks rocks rocks and tossed them into the noisy tumbler back home.

The reason anyone would tumble rocks in the first place is simple: when an ordinary stone is placed into the tumbler for a period of time and when the polishing process is complete, the stone is remarkably different than it was when the tumbling began.

The dirt gets washed off, but more, the rough edges are worn and broken away and ultimately it is smooth and clean, a better version of itself. Not a metamorphosis, not a changing of its essence, not even stronger *per se*, for this process is not about strength but rather about beauty and polish and shine.

A polished stone is more fascinating, more magnificent than it was before its polishing. Occasionally a stone comes out of the tumbler and it is *extraordinary,* other-worldly.

The process of rock tumbling is simple, though not quick.

There are two main kinds of rock tumblers, rotary and vibratory. I am told most people who tumble rocks use a rotary tumbler. One simply places his rocks into the rubber barrel of the tumbler, adds tumbling grit and water, and then lets her rip. Turn on the machine then get out of the way so the tumble-and-grit can do their work.

Now, if a person wants to achieve optimum smooth and shine in his tumbling, a four-step process is preferable – coarse grind, medium grind, fine grind, and then polish. Each of these steps takes about a week, so the whole mechanism runs upwards of a month long.

I read that people who want superbly shaped stones will run their rocks in only the coarse grit for up to four weeks.

A key element in Christianity is *water,* but might I add a little *grit* to the equation? Water cleanses the dirt and rinses the smut of living a real life and acknowledges the hope that one can be clean again. I will probably get dirty tomorrow, maybe even dirtier than today, but in matters of faith, there's plenty of water to go around.

Plenty of mercy and grace, daily washing and forgive your brother seventy times seven. Add confess your sins one to another to the equation and you will be healed, with hope for a cleaner tomorrow.

Life adds the grit, the irritants, the unavoidable dirt that comes from stepping outside your own door every day and knowing that either someone will make your life harder and dirtier or you will simply do that work yourself. This sovereign God of ours allows the course grit, even adds it Himself to the tumbler and often allows us to tumble for a long time.

I guess He is interested in superbly-shaped smooth stones.

The truth is simple; as a tumbling stone myself, I often don't trust fate or the universe or God or the government or my family with my life and I don't appreciate the simile, thank you very much. I don't cotton to this constant adding of the grit and irritant for extended periods of time, washing, refining, rubbing, washing again.

I suppose it's the tumbling itself I hate. That feeling of falling, the sense of existential dread, the wondering if I will finally find my balance again. Will I survive this and if so, is there actually any hope I'll come out shining, clean, or is rubbed raw the best I can hope for?

Dread feels like tumbling, sliding down a deep well, bumping hard against all sides. I grab at things, footholds and crevices in the stone to keep from falling farther, falling faster, but all of those things prove a tease, it seems; they hold us up for a moment or two, but eventually they break and fall and we are Humpty Dumpty once more, like we were already pretty sure would happen in the first place. And nobody can put us back together again.

When we are tumbling, we know one simple thing and only one – it's not over yet.

More grit. More water. More tumbling. *Things* are not enough to hold onto. I need a person. A Person.

For me, this gritty tumbling feels a bit like being *chased.*

I watched this video of an English bloke getting chased up a tree by a fierce and bellowing stag with a huge rack of horns on his head. The Englishman is on a walk and encounters the stag and simply stands too close. It happens sometimes, we get too close to danger, too near the stove. The stag grows increasingly agitated and starts charging the man, chasing him until there is simply nothing left for the man to do but to climb up the tree and wait it out. The woman narrating the video says she will call the police, but we never get to see the rescue. The video ends with the hollering Englishman stuck in the tree and the irritated stag honking and mewling and pawing the ground and the narrator crying for help.

But no help comes.

That's how dread feels, like being chased up a tree and being stuck there for a while, until either the stag gets bored and leaves or someone comes to help you. Which, as we know, can often take a very long time.

Sometimes we have to sit in the tree for a while and ride the storm out. Sometimes the strong, careless winds toss us down from our perches, and then a stag shows up again and we have to scramble back up to the top branches and shake our fists at the winds.

W*hy?* Why must there be so much falling and tumbling and chasing and grit? Is this necessary? Is this really what it takes to be superbly shaped?

I suppose it is.

An ordinary stone is a good and fine thing. A little muddy, rough around the edges, brown, plain.

But when an ordinary stone has been tumbled, rolled and rolled for an extended period of time with more and more grit added intentionally by the craftsman, when *this* stone is finished tumbling, the end result is extraordinary. Better, more beautiful, more smooth. Extraordinary.

Water to cleanse. Grit to smooth. Tumbling to work out the imperfections. This, I surmise, is the awful, awesome working of God in our lives.

To which I can only say, Thanks be to God.

When Winter Comes

It is winter. The chill bites and my bones rattle in frosty winds and today I cannot hear the songbird. Places North have snows deep and ice hard, but here in the South it's just cold, and not even *that cold*, but cold enough for us. Logs snap and crackle in my fireplace and I am well-bundled.

I know my breed is rare, but I love winter with its sharp crispness. I am made for the cold. I long for it in late October after the first teasing frost, yet every time I am surprised and feel tricked and disappointed when the cold is not yet ready to stay.

Indeed, there are those of us who love the bright sting of frigid air on warm skin and the frosty breaths on too-cold mornings. And I am aware of the science, the literal; winter nights are long and cold because the earth spins and tilts and the suns' rays are less direct, and gloved, red-scarved schoolgirls skip rosy-cheeked into school and we all watch our steps on slippery paths. Winter asks us to be a bit more careful.

It is the figurative winter that surprises me, shocks me even though I've read a'plenty and seen enough to forget not its inevitable coming. I have known times of barrenness and darkness when I felt reality fall cold onto my soul like unexpected ice, and yet still I wonder Why me? and Why now? When the nights are long, I cannot see what is coming. I do not *want* to see what is coming.

I have seen enough to know the other side of the bright moon is dark.

What then am I to do with winter if not embrace it, breathe it, feel its stings, and live its harsh moments? I understand things must die in order to live, but does that mean even *my* things? I think it must.

Must I pay attention to the cold days, to pry my sleepy eyes open and search under hard-frozen things for the beauty and the gifts? I think I must.

The active verbs required to move me, exhaust me – seek and find and search and work and pursue and dig and chase. I think I'd rather sit back and gaze into the metaphorical winter of my own discontent with a whimper rather than a bang.

Larry and I sit with our friend Sally as she eats her hospital lunch and forgets our names – it is her winter and she is bravely living every last minute of it as her earthly clock winds down. She tells funny stories and well-remembers the past but not the present. We smile and laugh and when we have to leave, she says *See you tomorrow, dahlin'* and returns to her Jello. She loves the lime Jello so the kind cafeteria-lady brings her two every afternoon.

Even winter has its sweet surprises if we are looking and not so angry at the cold that we are blind and can no longer pay attention.

Last week the church kids and I put on coats and hats and walked outside for a cold winter nature walk. I asked them to stay silent, I said we would hear and smell and see more if we could remain quiet. I must admit, I didn't think they were up to it, but they managed the silence like champs. We smelled the winter, heard its crackle and crunch and witnessed the death of things, we dipped ungloved hands hard into near-frozen water and *felt the season,* and the children grew even more silent in the awe of it, the gift of it.

We will walk again in the cold, the church kids and me, and I wonder if we will be a bit sad when winter wanes.

The cold winter strips away pretense and reveals the raw side of things. Southern winters are brief; humid warmth and foliage will arrive soon and cover what's been uncovered. While it's cold, I need to take a long look at the skeletal nakedness, before things are enveloped again in green and harder to see.

The solstice is past, the days are lengthening. Soon enough, the earth will toil and spin again and spring will arrive. The church kids and I heard the twitter of a songbird at the end of our walk yesterday. I tell them of what the Psalmist said, It was You who set all the boundaries of the earth; You made *both* summer and winter. We will go back inside and draw some pictures and try to make a bit of sense of it all.

But while I am here in winter's cold raw grasp, I need to pay attention, turn over a cold stone, or a cold heart, and dare to take a look at what's underneath.

This is the day the Lord has made, the least I can do is to unbundle and feel it. Maybe then I will rejoice and be glad.

The quiet moments between things can be the dearest, then moments after and before.

Lo, I Am With You Always...

You always think you'll be able to see these things coming. The tree before it falls, the harsh and hurtful word, the widening crack before the relationship crumbles completely. The too-bright lights of the speeding car barreling toward you in your lane. But, ah, there are always surprises.

After he hit me head-on, there were many quiet moments. Moments before the nurse with the phone tapped on the driver's side window and before the arrival of the ambulance and the firemen with the Jaws-of-Life. Moments when I could hear the faint *whoosh-whoosh* of Medevac helicopter blades looking for a landing place amidst tall trees on old Germantown Parkway and wondered if that sound could possibly be for me.

There was no pain, not yet. Just quiet on a cold, snowy, January night in Memphis.

The quiet moments between things can be the dearest, then moments after and before.

The quiet moments after the nurse called for the ambulance and brought a blanket from her trunk because the little bit of snow falling was coming inside the wreck of my well-crumpled car and dusting my legs I could not move. You're in shock, were the words she said but they didn't make much sense to me at the time. I didn't know what those words meant.

The quiet moments before my parents arrived at the scene – my mother with her nurse face (*how can I help?*) and my father with his teary daddy face (*is that really my baby-girl in that mangled mess?*).

The quiet moments before Buddy, the paramedic, arrived with the stretcher and the bandages and the morphine and the hope and his fabulously thick Southern drawl that lingers still in my memory for more than twenty-five years now, every single time I hear a siren whining its way through the city. "Now don't you worry none, missy. Me and the Jaws-of-Life here'll get you right outta there. You might have to drag yourself out the window a little bit, though. Shouldn't take long. You got strength left, can you help me, can you pull yourself out with your arms?"

These were the silent, slow, suspended moments in which I contemplated why I felt no fear. Perhaps it was my companions on this desperate winter night that carried the fear for me. *Lo, I am with you always* tapped patiently at the driver's side window, reminding me of his presence, and *Though I walk through the valley of the shadow of death, I will fear no evil, for You are with me* sat quietly, peacefully beside me in the front seat. *In my Father's house are many mansions* even made a fleeting cameo appearance beside me in the passenger seat of my mangled Honda as I slowly thought, Am I about to see God in Person, face to face? Is this what it feels like to be absent from the body?

Dream-like, surreal even, but no fear. Warm instead of cold. I guess, in my shock, I simply believed what I'd heard, that with God all things somehow work together for good. All will be well. If it were not so, He would have told us.

Some of my quiet thoughts were happy ones. I felt deep happiness that she was not riding with me that day. Her five-year-old's books and Barbies were in the ruined floorboard, but she was at her grandmother's. The door on her side of the car was now pushing hard against my right shoulder but she was not, and for that I was happy and I smiled an injured smile and thought of her playing dolls, safe on my mother's thick carpets.

I remember really hoping I would see her again, and her gentle father. Some of my quiet thoughts were full of wonder. I wondered what her life would be like without a mother. There is a somber quality to such a thought, heavy with the ripe weight of a life completely changed, something to ponder in the few moments before the ambulance arrived – but I remember no fear in these thoughts.

I wondered how he would cope and if he would marry again.

I wondered about Heaven. Was this God's voice I heard saying, *Peace, be still?* Was it an angel's song, a memory, a snippet of an old poem? Is this faith, is this the substance of things hoped for? Whatever happens, all is well?

Instead of going to Heaven that night, I went to the Baptist Hospital, the old one on Union Avenue which they've now demolished. The quiet moments in the dark car were replaced with the noisy cacophony of healing – beeping and tapping and shouts and whispers and papers to be signed and a police-woman needing a full report and prayers and a best-friend-who-is-a-doctor who couldn't quit crying which is never a good sign and foul-tasting liquids and batteries of tests.

Surgeries three, like weird sisters.

Healing instead of Heaven, for the time being. There are things still to be done here and Heaven can wait. I am wife and mother and daughter and sister and teacher and friend, so I'll stay here and do this work for a while longer.

Years have passed, almost three decades now, and pain's intensity is long since misremembered. Nothing left of that evening but my pensive thoughts and plenty of scars, clean surgical reminders that we must fight hard for this life.

What remains deepest is the memory of the silent moments where I heard the voice of God in the depths of quiet. I can hear it still, if I can be quiet, if I am listening.

The Old Man & The Young Boy

The girl's return to the woods was unplanned. Her father's funeral had undone her.

It's easier when you know it's coming, the townspeople had said to her for the past few weeks, but the townspeople were wrong. Slow demise is still demise, and death, when it bites, is no respecter of persons – its teeth always sharp. The girl had come to the woods to be alone with her book-of-words; weary of both comfort and company, she longed to hear the creek and the sparrows again, and she tarried long on the warm rock, listening for truth in the wind's soft voice.

And she wrote.

In her book-of-words, just above the photograph of her father as a young man, she'd written *The Lord gives and the Lord takes away* in strong letters, and she'd jotted down the lyrics of the creek's passionate love song, lyrics she'd heard and sung throughout her childhood.

The sun cooled, and the girl turned toward home; it was rude to stay out so long with so many visitors in town for the funeral. But halfway to her house she realized she'd left the woods without her book-of-words, she'd left her book behind on the large rock. So, she reentered the woods at a faster pace, for the second time in the same afternoon, more frenzied than the time before.

The book was not on the large rock by the creek. I *must* have left it here, she said out loud to the trees, for I didn't sit anywhere else. She searched beside the great stone but found nothing, save the small mounding of the night creatures. The girl kicked the leaves around the creek bank and searched in panic around trees nowhere near the stone, but her worn book-of-words was lost and seemed determined to be so.

This day had defeated her again.

Can we help you? whispered a voice behind her. The girl started in alarm. Turning, she saw an unusual pair standing behind her, close to the water – a very old man and a very young boy. They were holding hands. Can we help you? the old man repeated in an ancient whisper, and the young boy nodded with a shy smile.

I've lost my words, the girl said and began to cry. Ah, yes. The old man paused. Is that all you've lost today? he whispered.

No, the girl whispered in return, not all.

The boy kicked at the grass around the large stone, and the birds filled the silence with their soft song.

This little boy here don't say much, the old man offered, he ain't got his words yet. He just got here not too long ago. The old man scratched his bald head. And I'm pretty much done with talking myself, looks like, but I guess me and him are pretty content with things for the most part.

The telling of his own story brought him a smile. My father's funeral was today, the girl said.

The old man nodded and said nothing and the little boy smiled.

I wasn't ready for it, even though he'd been sick a very long time, the girl admitted. The creek gurgled, and the man and the boy said nothing.

I wrote all about it in my book-of-words, the girl whispered. I've written everything for the last year there, and now it's gone too. Then the girl put her face in her hands and wept hot, sad, angry tears.

The old man and the young boy stood still and said nothing, but the birds kept singing nonetheless.

After a while the old man said, A little earlier, me and the little boy seen your book floating down the creek. Must've fallen in when you rose up to go home. The little boy here jumped in the creek and tried to grab it, but it had already moved into the fast, deep water. Anyway, he was too little to fetch it and I am too old to swim. We tried, did what we could, but we couldn't save your treasure.

It's a mighty great loss, the girl said.

Yes, the old man agreed. The loss of one's words is maybe the greatest loss of all. I been feeling mine fading for a while now, and the little boy here, well, he ain't got his yet. The boy patted the old man's hand.

It was quiet for a long spell before the girl spoke again. Well, I guess I'd better head on home, she said. I've been gone long enough, everyone will worry. As she turned to leave, the old man spoke, I reckon there's one thing as important as words, maybe even more so.

What is that? the girl asked.

Can you tell her, boy? the old man asked.

The little boy plucked a tiny purple flower from the edge of the creek, his thin fingers damp and cold from the water. He put the flower to his ear for a long moment, listening, listening; finally, he gave the flower to the girl and opened his lips. In a voice as clear and sparkling as the creek's water, the little boy sang the secret song of the flower, and the rocks joined in and then the trees and then the wind and then the birds, all singing the sweet song of the woods, the song of deepest memory – the song written long before the boy's time or the old man's time; the song existed before time began at all. The air was sweet and strong with the harmony of Nature's ancient music.

The girl closed her eyes in deference to the majestic. As the boy's pristine voice faded, she opened her eyes and dared ask her final question. For whose delight did the flower bloom and the creek and the boy sing, and why did the rocks and stones and trees join in the singing?

The old man spoke his last words in a whisper so soft the girl thought it was the breath of the wind. Memory may be our greatest gift, perhaps better than all the words in all the languages, the old man said. When you lose your words, hold fast to your memories, for they are your sustenance. And the song? Nature sings her most beautiful song for the listener, the one who comes with ears to hear.

And without a good-bye, the very old man and the very young boy turned and walked out of sight deep into the dark of the woods.

And the girl, her book-of-words lost forever, took the memory of her father out of the woods with her and carried it deep within her for the rest of her days.

And it sustained her.

Schadenfreude

I am so tired of *schadenfreude.*

I'm on a long walk with my walkaholic husband and the dog. The Memphis temps are moderate for February. Bikers and walkers and joggers and kids on scooters are everywhere. A few convertibles make their topless debuts, and dogs of every variety bark their doggy-joy in the unexpected sunshine. A very young child, a boy, quick-leaves his bat and ball and runs across his yard to pet our mutt Joe, and the boy's father grins at his son's bravery from behind home plate.

I witness the beginnings of buds on trees, making their prodigious plumpness known, though still timid of winter's bite, but almost ready, ever hopeful. The green daffodil leaves along my garden walk peek upward, the beginnings of their spring stretching – I see hints of yellow there but still just hints. Winter will return, it's early February, but a warm day reminds us of all things good, all things happy.

So, on a day like this, I can quite forget how tired I am of *schadenfreude.*

These days my favorite novelist is Fyodor Dostoevsky – who knows what tomorrow may bring.

Dostoevsky speaks of *schadenfreude* although he doesn't use the word as such. In his novel *Crime and Punishment,* the woman Pulcheria is in a destitute place. Pulcheria's daughter Dunya is preparing to marry a wretched, egotistical man for money in order to save her own family from poverty, and there seems to be nothing Pulcheria or anyone else can do to stop this marriage.

Dunya is determined to do this thing, noble or ignoble, it's hard to know.

At this point in the narrative, a prostitute named Sonya enters the scene and it is here the reader witnesses *schadenfreude.* A woman far more destitute than Pulcheria and Dunya, Sonya is dressed in the ostentatious garb of the Russian prostitute of 1860, so everyone knows what she's been up to.

Here's how the text reads: *Pulcheria Alexandrovna glanced at Sonya, and slightly narrowed her eyes. In spite of her embarrassment before her son's urgent and challenging look, Pulcheria could not deny herself that satisfaction.*

Pulcheria-the-Impoverished is quietly glad to see Sonya-the-Prostitute in such dire straits, even looking down her nose and lowering her eyes at her in pleasure, because Sonya's situation enables Pulcheria to feel better about herself.

Sometimes, when someone has a worse time of things than we do, we feel glad because we then feel better about ourselves and our situation – this is *schadenfreude.*

And I have grown so tired of it.

Surely other ways to live exist. Grander, higher paths.

Rejoice with those who rejoice and weep with those who weep comes to mind. What a beautiful way to choose to live, so holy this calling to the repetition of selflessness. Compassion with a healthy dose of empathy. Why, oh why, won't I choose this lovely walkway? Is the choice to rejoice and weep alongside my human companions really that difficult?

But we so often miss it, addicted we are to the momentary shudder of relief that is *schadenfreude.*

Schadenfreude is just the opposite of this holy calling. With *schadenfreude,* we rejoice when others fall and can grow angry or at least jealous when good fortune befalls another. We are hooked on the delight we find in others' misfortune, and this is the ugly ugly ugly opposite of peaceful living.

Yet society is full of it, social media reeks of it, television thrives on it. We *love* to see the fall of someone else because it means, for the moment, the fall is not ours.

At the time of this writing, Brian Williams comes to mind, and anybody and everybody else who falls from grace in this too-often graceless culture of ours. I don't know all the details of Williams' story of "remembering" or "misremembering" his helicopter trip, and I am of course interested in proper and truthful reporting (or I used to be before I stopped watching the nightly news).

But what Dostoevsky portrays in fiction, I daily watch unfold in fact: people love to watch the fall of a man because for a minute, they then feel better about themselves.

Research finds that people of low self-esteem are more likely to feel *schadenfreude* than those with high self-esteem – that rings true to me. Someone to mock and scorn, someone to look down on and gossip about, *schadenfreude* is almost irresistible.

I've grown so very tired of it, haven't you?

Perhaps silence is a respite from *schadenfreude*. I might not be able to stop the frenzied, selfish noise of the world, but I *can* control my own listening to it.

Turning the media off, closing the door to the Internet. I have control of this. Sitting still and comfortable in the silence of the room where I read and on the paths where I walk. Feeling the unexpected warmth of the sun on my face on a February afternoon, stopping long enough to *really feel it.*

Walking alongside a student who weeps, a friend who grieves. Quiet walking, not talk-walking, advice-giving, fixing, judging, worrying, fretting sorts of walking. Just plain old walking alongside and listening. Helping someone who will never help me in return.

Living smaller and quieter is helping me more than I ever thought possible.

I am trying to distance myself from *schadenfreude,* I want no part of it. I think this is what Jesus did. The people didn't understand his position, but He didn't seem to mind nor did He make excuses for His decision.

I sit in quiet now to write, to listen to February birds sing noisy in the dawn. I envy them, for there seems to be no *schadenfreude* in the natural world. Just birds and squirrels and gophers and moles building and creating and singing and chirping.

There is danger and death in the natural world, make no mistake, but no *schadenfreude.* No gladness of others' misfortune.

What a fine state in which to dwell, a state in which I am trying to live more and more.

ON BEING STYMIED

I haven't written anything since my father died.

No, that's hyperbole. I've written so many things since my father died – hundreds of sentence pieces, bits and fragments live slant on the insides of all my books, rough beasts waiting for their time to come round at last. Virgin nouns spend lazy days at their windows, pining for mates, watching and praying at the highways and hedges, some even have their lamps trimmed but most are unprepared when the bridegroom verbs appear. Word clusters litter the cool lakebed of my winter purse, index cards and paper scraps bulge with phrases un-bloomed, still in their ninth-month. Nothing worthy seems coming.

When my father died, I wanted to write something beautiful about death, something grand, seminal, and in particular, I felt the need to write something important about the death of a good man, a very good man. I wanted noble words, poignant and memorable and apt and smart and rich and fresh, but all the metaphors seemed to fade just before delivery and images arrived stillborn.

It is hard to find birth in death; there's no delivery room at the funeral home. How can two polar things peacefully live together when both vie so vehemently for the attention of the immediate? When something dies – a person, a job, a friendship, a marriage, a dream – all we have left are the memories of the thing, good and bad. Like our universe, memory expands in all directions, swirling and moving, unreliably, at the speed of thought. Changing with every capricious retelling, story evolves as time barrels through space, and when you hear even your own tale told twenty years later, it's not the same story at all, but much better, or much worse. Even when story is written down, no longer to be changed, meaning rests in the reader's fragile interpretation and again, who knows what side of the bed she woke up on?

Who dares to touch such a thing?

I have written nothing substantial in a long time, nothing I dare to share, for several months, far too long. And it is not for lack of effort, I'm sad to report. Four essay beginnings sit like hard stumps on my screen, the one entitled "An Hour Badly Spent" beckons me every single morning, begging to be birthed or at least given a chance, but alas, I have to wonder if I've become afraid.

I sometimes think I read too many great writers, for my writing withers in their presence, and I've grown weary of the comparison. Self-doubt is hard, stony ground to till.

Water is required for birth and growth, and digging must

happen for a new thing to be planted. I have felt the hard ground and know its infertility; being stymied and stuck is a place from which to escape.

The desert gives birth to nothing but the ugly twins of worry and angst, brutish children who only take and never give.

What does one *do* when she finds herself stymied, and who hasn't found herself sitting among dry leaves in a dry time? The loss of last season's crop was so painful and the winter so long, who is brave enough to believe in spring?

A certain vision appears to me in dream, and I jump from my bed and snatch up the pencil; I must write this down before it flits away, teasing, like mist or memory. The question must come before the answer:

What must we do to be saved?

Believe.

Stand up, walk, don't sit back down until you have walked a little longer than usual.

Pray, say the words out loud.

Pick up a pen and write the letter you've waited too long to write.

Ask for forgiveness. Give forgiveness.

Grieve. Talk about it.

Write down your biggest worry on a piece of paper and then burn it in the fire. I realize it's a metaphor, but it feels good anyway.

If you have made a mistake, fix it. If you can't fix it, live with it. You are not dead yet, so live.

Quit complaining. Get a therapist.

Quit gossiping. Try, even for just one quick hour.

Give someone a real compliment.

Get a job. Get a new job. Decide to like the job you have and then do it well.

Turn off the television. Turn off the television. Turn off the television.

Put down the phone. Put down the phone. Put down the phone. Now pick the phone back up and make that call you've been avoiding; the call you wish you didn't have to make but know you should. Do it today.

Read something.

Write something.

Give something away. Give something to a person dealing with homelessness without questioning his motive; someone important said it is better to give than to receive, and He was right. The gift is in the giving.

Kiss a baby.

Smile.

Do it all again.

Writer, I shout to myself in the cold, sleepless hours, you are not dead yet, so get up and live! Stand up this morning and start to write again. Set down your visions of grandeur and pick up your sheer ordinariness, your own words, not the words of Annie or Ann or Flannery or Eudora or Zadie or Marilynne or Joan or Maya or Sylvia or Charlotte or Virginia or Toni or Jane or Harper or Zora or Willa or Jhumpa or Amy or Donna or Barbara.

I respect the hard ground and now know that my vast hubris hardens and heavies, rather than lightens, my load. It is time to dig again and the overwhelming fear of it subsides as I pick up my pen – I'll dig with it. And good, decent words will be my seed. And I will water it all with tears.

Now I know, things grow again.

Good Food Mike

Difficult people can get lost.

My uncle Mike was a difficult person, a fact that wasn't too hard for me to bear because I didn't see him all that much, but a fact excruciating for my mother. These two grew up together in a spectacularly abusive home and shared the measured bondage of rage and alcohol, which are, of course, fierce bedfellows. Add poverty to the mix and you've got yourself a triple threat, a messy recipe for disaster.

On my mother's wedding day (just barely eighteen and ready to get the heck out of there), her brother Mike comes to her bedside (eleven and too young yet to plan his escape) and wakes her up. On his knees he is. Praying? Pleading? Begging. Please don't get married today, sissy. If you get married and leave me here, I'll be the saddest boy in Mississippi. Who will make my breakfast toast and pack my lunch for school? he weeps.

One does not forget things like this.

Little Boy Mike grew up and became Grown-Up Mike.

It is no surprise to anyone when the child of two profound alcoholics grows up to be one as well. We all know what the studies say about these things; twenty-five percent of children of alcoholics become alcoholics themselves...God, help us.

As a kid, though, I thought my Uncle Mike was really cool.

It was the 1970's and Mike lived in a Colorado commune and drank Red Zinger Tea and sat on mountaintops with his terrifically groovy girlfriend. We visited him once when I was about fifteen and my brother was about twelve, and we were quite enamored of his life – my brother and I, I mean. My parents, not so much.

We sat on a mountaintop with snow peaks in the background, even in the summer, but what impressed me most was that Mike and his girlfriend had equally long hair. She wore cool long skirts and brought a picnic basket filled to the brim with what my father called "Colorado hippie food," granola, hummus, sprouts, so different from the Southern Baptist food we ate in Tennessee, which includes but is not limited to fried pickles, fried potatoes, fried pies, fried chicken, chicken-fried steak, and fried vegetables of all makes and models.

My brother and I talked about Red Zinger Tea for a long time after that that visit to Colorado; we still do sometimes.

When Mike finally left the commune, he became a fine chef, self-taught from his mother's Delta-Cajun handwritten recipes. Mike did all the cooking for my wedding after-party, my birthday extravaganza at my parents' house. (Yes, I got married on my birthday.) Mike was not drinking that night, trying to be a good uncle for the wedding. He carved swans out of squashes and elegant sandwiches with cucumbers and fancy aioli and no crusts. He was the chef-in-charge of my big, fat, fun, wedding-birthday party, and people said things like, Are you a chef? and I didn't know your uncle was such a great cook and You should consider opening a catering business!

Mike cheffed for a while at a country club in Memphis where wealthy people gave him great tips and encouraged him to open his own business. You really could do this! they'd say. There were good nights, nights of clean starched white coats and stiff tall chef hats that smelled of lemon and garlic and the beginnings of respect. Pleased brides and their mothers cooed and Mike's own nieces and nephews renamed him Good-Food-Mike! and jumped with pleasure when he was around to cook for them.

What grace, what hope there is in a new name.

But too many bad nights simply outweighed the good.

Demons from Good-Food-Mike's haunted past would not stop chasing him down lonely, dirt roads, those same demons that spurred Mike's drunk daddy to chase him and his sister and mother down a dark Mississippi road on a hot night, the scariest night of anyone's life, the night daddy brought a butcher knife on his chase. Scary fathers and demons-in-dreams too often tip the scales and the bad simply becomes heavier than the good and the terrified little boy has to go somewhere so he just keeps running and hiding in bottles.

Shadows and their substance.

Uncle Mike lived with my parents off and on for many years. They gave him a car and he disappeared and it took several days before they found him and the wrecked car, floorboard laden with empty vodka bottles, all down in the brown water of a drainage ditch. Slow death by excess, an American commentary.

My father said Mike, if you are going to live with us, please don't smoke in the house, and Mike said Of course, I would never smoke in your house but he did anyway and fell asleep in bed with a lit cigarette and nearly set the house on fire.

Sometimes there are last straws and choices that finally break the strong backs of camels.

If rescue missions had point systems, my Uncle Mike would have claimed platinum card status in no time flat. A frequent flyer he was, in and out of the best-of-the-best missions throughout the Southeast. One remarkable thing about my Uncle Mike, a man of genuine talent, was he always dared to leave his mark; he painted the murals on the mission walls at the Calvary Rescue Mission and the Bible verses on the mission canvasses at the Union Mission; he sang a pure and strong tenor line to all the hymns played by volunteer hands on old tinny pianos. Surely Good-Food-Mike set the world record for the number of burgers flipped on mission grills.

But Mike's sojourns always ended the same unfortunate way, with him flying all too frequently out the door, into the street, and back to the bottle. He always found his message in a bottle, finding what would be better lost.

Grown-Up-Homeless-Bottled Uncle Mike finally left Memphis to live in a mission in Jackson, Mississippi, which ended up easier for everybody, though it always left my mother weepy and quiet when he called. My mother cried years of tears over her little brother, Good-Food-Mike.

And He took the five loaves, and the two fishes, and looking up to heaven, he blessed, and brake, and gave the loaves to his disciples, and the disciples to the multitude.

The Son of God came to feed the hungry and restore the broken. Evidently so did Brother Rosco at the men's rescue mission.

A small miracle – is there such a thing? – happened at Brother Rosco's mission that had not occurred at any of the other missions or on any of the park benches or bus stations or homeless shelters of my uncle's checkered history.

Mike's small miracle did not include walking on Gulf Coast water nor turning loaves and fishes into fried chicken and catfish. Mike's miracle was a quieter one but no less miraculous. Under Brother Rosco's care, Mike simply settled in. Maybe he just got tired of running, but Mike unpacked and allowed himself to dare to be loved and fed and restored by one who came to seek and save the lost, a man named Rosco, a savior with dirty fingernails and seemingly endless patience for men in bottles.

At Brother Rosco's patient urging, Good-Food-Mike began to cook fine meals for the mission men, not just burgers and hotdogs but complicated country club menus of sandwiches with fancy mayonnaise and swans made out of squashes and roasted red pepper hummus and herbed chicken on the grill. Lunches and dinners peppered with grace and care and attention to detail. Food fit for, kings?

Then one day the men started calling my uncle "Chef." Oh, the importance of a name, and a new name to boot! What hope, what promise, what newness of future the old patriarch must have felt when God said, Your name is no longer Jacob. From now on it is Israel; you've wrestled with God and you've come through.

Does Newly-Named-Mike dare to feel this ancient kinship, does he dare to slowly inhale this unexpected breath of self-respect in the warm and humid Mississippi breezes, something brand new? I think he does. It comes slowly, as most things do in the sultry Mississippi heat, but it does come.

And Jesus said unto them, I am the bread of life: he that cometh to me shall never hunger; and he that believeth on me shall never thirst.

Redemptive, peaceful years passed, a goodly number of them, cooking and eating and living beside Rosco-the-Restorer. Chef Mike made seafood gumbo from a New Orleans recipe he found in his mother's dilapidated cookbook. Bits of crab and crawfish occasionally made their way to the men's mission, as did meringues and shrimp dip and chicken-fried chicken. Bottles replaced by manna from a Mississippi heaven, and manna's companion is hope. So goes the story.

Good-Food-Mike, up to his elbows in kitchen grease and flour and government cheese and regret, but his heart alive again with new-found respect unexpected. The steady return of faith sprinkled with a touch of respect, slow-cooked over open flames.

And they that did eat of the loaves were about five thousand men. Loaves and fishes broken for the broken.

There were plenty of hard times still. Month after month when Mike called my mother and said, I'm leaving this mission. I'm better now, I'm not drinking anymore, and I'm getting out of here. I'm better than this, these people around here are all losers, and month after month my mother begged him to stay, You're doing so well there, Chef, who will cook for the men if you leave? What about the gumbo and the chocolate-chip cookies and the homemade sour dough bread? Don't give up. stay, please stay.

He stayed.

One day my mother received a phone call from Brother Rosco, who said in a small, still voice, I have very sad news for you. Chef died today. Everyone cried.

I spoke at Mike's funeral, as did my brother. We laughed and reminisced about the Red Zinger Tea and the hippie food as we sat in the stiff wooden pews of the funeral home chapel in the sweltering early summer heat.

The chapel was far from full. A few of my parents' friends made the trip from Memphis and about eight men from the Jackson mission came in, straight from the over-heat of the un-air-conditioned mission van. Sweaty men who were serious-acting and all wore coats and ties for the occasion. Men on a mission.

My brother spoke hope and reminded the small gathering that God's redemption is for everyone, and we all said Amen, that's right. I recalled what Lord Tennyson said in similar circumstances, when his dearest friend Arthur Hallam died:

I hold it true, whate'er befall;
I feel it, when I sorrow most;
'Tis better to have loved and lost
Than never to have loved at all.

and all said, Amen, that's right, too. But when Brother Rosco stood to speak, we heard the plain-spoken, gentle voice of God. Brothers and Sisters, here are some of the men whose lives were touched by Mike. Men, which of you would like to stand today and tell Chef's sister about the last years of his life?

The used-to-be-homeless stood to speak, one man straightening his unaccustomed tie, shuffling his newly-shod feet, Chef made me food like I never tasted before. One time he made us some herb butter for our bread. I didn't know there was food like that. He treated me like a king.

Another man said, Chef kept homemade chocolate-chip cookies and candy in his room for all us men. Ain't nobody never done that for me before.

A tall elegant-looking man with newly-shined shoes said shyly, Mike was my teacher. He done helped me to learn to read. I learned to read the Bible. At the conclusion of his eulogy, this man knelt down a bit and looked my mother square in the face and said with unexpected authority, Your brother changed my life.

Dignity where there had been none. Love breathing life into the ashes of failure like leaven in a loaf. The soft silence is our music.

We drove down the dusty red-dirt roads to the country cemetery together, just a couple of cars of us. The mission van arrived a bit late, stirring anew the red dust after its settle. My brother said a few more words, *Surely goodness and mercy shall follow me all the days of my life, and I shall dwell in the house of the*

Lord forever. My sweet father, who helped Mike for so many years with so little hope, said some thankful brother-in-law words to God and to Brother Rosco. The service concluded and we all rose to move toward hugs and home when Brother Rosco reminded his quiet men, Brothers, don't you have something for Chef's sister?

The tall, shy, elegant man with the shiny shoes scooted forward on the dusty green-felt funeral carpet and produced a bouquet of fresh daisies magician-like from behind his back, supermarket price tag still stuck to one of the white daisy petals, unnoticed by the giver. He knelt before my mother and presented the daisies to her with that same quiet dignity. Ma'am, he began. Sorry we was a minute late. We put our money together and got you these at the Snappy Sacker store. We wanted to get some flowers for the sister of the man who saved us. He fed us all, stomach and soul.

There's a lad here which hath five barley loaves and two small fishes. But what are they among so many?

A drop in the bucket. Looks like it only takes a drop for those who dare to believe.

ADVENT

The Christmas Star

On December 21, 2020, Jupiter overtook Saturn for what astronomers called the "Great Conjunction." The two largest planets in our solar system lined up into what appeared as one grand star in the cold winter sky.

According to the Royal Astronomical Society, conjunctions this close are quite unusual. Jupiter and Saturn were last seen in such proximity in 1623, but on that occasion, the two planets were close to the sun and would have been difficult, if not impossible, to see. The last time Jupiter and Saturn were this close and so easy to see was in 1226, almost 400 years before Galileo first pointed his telescope skyward and saw mountains and craters on the moon, as well as the miraculous rings around Saturn and four of Jupiter's moons. Oh my, what joy to be the *first* to see such a sight!

Since nearly 800 years have passed since these two grand planets dared dance this close, the least I could do is show up to watch.

Every evening for a week leading up to the big event, I stood outside in my cold street and gazed up into the clear air, and with a pair of binoculars perched on my nose, I watched Jupiter and Saturn grow closer and closer together.

Why have I not bought a telescope? I thought of my good friend Orion, who died several years back, and how he dragged his fine telescope onto the soccer field at our school on cold winter nights and knew exactly where to point it into the night sky for friends and students who braved the cold to come and take a peek at glory and how glad I am that I dragged my husband and ten-year-old daughter out there, even when it was just the four of us, especially then, and listened as Orion told us in his low and husky voice about his love affair with the stars and the infinite sky.

The night of the conjunction, though, something happened I hadn't expected. The astronomers said that Jupiter would overtake Saturn low on the early evening horizon, but I had not understood quite how low that would be. On December 21 at dusk, I went outside to find the planets descending below the suburban tree tops, out of my view. I live in a neighborhood with very tall, old trees; I had not accounted for the trees.

Despair is the impetus for creativity. In one unanimous impulse, I and my fellow watchers – my across-the-street neighbors, a couple of kin-folk, and two little kids – scrambled up to the tiptop of my roof where we could see in clear view the two bright planets join together on the evening horizon. We stood there for a long while, silent in the cold, as close as we could get to the sky.

The next great conjunctions will occur on November 2, 2040, I plan to be around for this one, and April 7, 2060, I'm pretty sure I'll miss this one. But you never know. Perhaps some great-grand-child will wheel me out onto the lawn of my retirement village and shout in my deaf ear to look up. *Granny, don't forget to look up!* I hope this is exactly what happens.

The newspapers called the December 2020 conjunction "the Christmas Star." And as full of wonder as it was, this phenomenon has happened before and will happen again. The star of Bethlehem, though, according to Ignatius of Antioch, was something entirely other: "It shone forth in heaven brighter than all the stars; its light was indescribable, its strangeness caused amazement. All the rest of the constellations, together with the sun and moon, formed a chorus around the star, yet the star itself far outshone them all, and there was perplexity about the origin of this strange phenomenon, which was so unlike the others."

What I witnessed from my rooftop was worth every effort, quite remarkable in its wonder and mathematical predictability, but not the only-once-in-history star of Bethlehem. Can you imagine the celestial wonder that must have been, a star so bright it moved both men and angels to leave their homelands and travel extravagant distances to proclaim its other-worldly message?

I'd like to see that. Maybe one day.

What the Star Sees

Bright Star, would I were steadfast as thou art – John Keats

Since the second day of Creation, the stars have stood aloft, silent steadfast watchers of the night sky. What a wonder to consider what they have witnessed through the millennia. Perhaps the bright Christmas star has seen the most, she who has the stories to tell, she who can provide glimpses and snatches of meaning within the blurry eons of murky human movement.

She who watched a pregnant, teenage girl trudge on foot and bounce on mule, toiling heavy toward a city foreign to her, one called Bethlehem, to find No Vacancy her only greeting and mere barn animals to low and bleat and proclaim and sing to her newborn His first lullaby. And at this baby's first cries, the star watched as two different types of men – both knowledgeable and learned concerning the comings-and-goings of the stars, both having studied stars and lived with stars in their respective fields – these men moving from different places and stations toward the same place on those first nights, this tiny village called Bethlehem, journeying with crown and gift and lamb and staff and perfume and gold, drawn as one to One, to the brightness of something new.

And angel voices, cherubim and seraphim, warming up, tuning, piercing the night sky, opening the darkness of millennia past and future to sing the long-awaited song of hope – the promise of life and life and life to come. Did the star move as well, adjust metaphysically or metaphorically to actually house herself above a lowly, Jewish stable, did she shift her eternal spot to sit above a manger, to guide and watch?

It seems the Christmas story is about journey, movement, pilgrims trekking along love-paths from here to there with meager gifts in hand and hope in heart, the hope of seeing the miraculous. Pilgrims like my brother, Santa-clad, his Santa-bag filled to spilling, trekking out late, so so late, way past bedtime on Christmas Eve to the door of a family whose Christmas most needed a miraculous visit, stress-pressed with grief, turned away from belief toward unbelief. Not all years are easy ones, but hope still knocks. A phone call, a Christmas card, a note sent for the first time in many years, a tiny step toward forgiveness, reconciliation, redemption, a first act of contrition – small movements dancing toward restoration. Someone takes the first dance step. And the star sees.

She watches the comings-and-goings of travelers. The journey that Christmas Eve to cold Wisconsin, my daughter's first Christmas in her new house, and the star and her brother the winter moon watch us, shine their bright lights for us as we slush down unfamiliar snowy roads, packages piled high in the backseat and Burl Ives' creamy crooning voice for miles and miles and miles of snow, and hot coffee and fur-lined boots for freezing toes for every pitstop from Tennessee to Missouri to Illinois to Wisconsin, reminding us that the journey is the best part of the gift. The star sees.

She watches o'er the overly busy – Romans building empires and post-modern-plural-relative folk doing the same, no time for worship, no pause no peace. The star knows that quiet does not connote lack of meaning, but most often just the opposite.

She saw the apartment complex we visited that Christmas when our daughter, then so young, asked why the babies had such messy legs and bottoms and looking we realized these babies born-of-poverty were diapered with the day's newspaper and Scotch tape, and Susie's angry, tearful drive to Walmart to buy every proper diaper those bulging shelves offered. The star sees all these things in too many places far too regularly.

And that coldest of winters when Sally and Larry, mother and son, met the young boy in that tumbledown Mississippi shack with no heat, winter wind cold-blowing through broken floorboards. And the boy's little sister, a stunned imprisoned child, locked in a cold, dark closet – forgotten was she? Two children hungry dirty lost, no parent in sight. Found them clothes and a proper place to stay. One child survives the nightmare of this upbringing and one does not. Does the star weep, watching this endless story over and over through the millennia?

I have nothing but questions. So much has she seen from her steadfast, lofty height while we are here below, longing for a little wisdom and guidance and knowledge and justice and understanding.

So I ask her. What happens to those babies, newspaper-clad? How will those without homes stay warm this winter if there are no blankets or sleeping bags brought? And the poor, the stunned children locked in forgotten closets? No Christmas gift, no salvation for them? What do I do when people refuse the dance steps of reconciliation? What if the note is never written, the phone number not dialed, forgiveness remains unasked-for? Is this world too broken? How can that be when there is also so much beauty? Beauty in ashes, hope unbloomed, how is it?

Her answer is soft, quiet – the stars don't yell, I'm told. Answers do come, but so often they arrive on a whiff, a breath, a thought swift-fleeting, missed if not listening closely. Paradox is at the root of the Christmas story, the star whispers. Wounded perfection, beauty coupled hand-in-hand with trouble. From the very beginning a homeless teenage Mother bore the Light in a darkened place, journeyed from known to unknown, carrying nothing with her but Hope.

Do what you can, is the star's soft answer. Take the steps, join the journey, and do what you can. Are you trying to be the active hands of God? she challenges me. The world is not too broken and joy does not lie slain. Are there no workhouses, no orphanages? a merciless man named Ebenezer once asked, pre-dreams, certainly not alone in the cruelty of this query. But he changed, he acted; indeed, the hearts of Scrooges do soften and Grinches' hearts can become large. So do not wait to do what you can. Prayers are still answered, though oft in ways as varied as the stars.

On the second day of Creation, the Lord made the stars, and the bright Christmas star has been watching aloft ever since, seeing the wondrous and the dreadful and the terrible beauty of it all. I open my eyes and my heart to accept the paradox and embrace the journey. I will try to say with Mary, *I am the Lord's servant, may it be to me as you have said.*

The pure in heart are blessed and see God because they want to, because they seek him, steadfastly, simply. I want to be pure in heart, I want to see God. It seems the Christmas story is about movement, journey, paths of love from there to here.

Mary did what she could, and I will try to do the same. And the silent star will see.

THIN SLIVER OF GLORY

The tornado warning on my phone roused me at 12:36 this morning, but it was the cacophonous chorus of tornado alarms, police sirens, and gigantic rolls of thunder that woke me fully. I lay still in my bed to listen.

Unless I force it shut, my bedroom door doesn't close completely, so in the pitch of night there's always a thin line of dim, yellow street light that slivers through the tiny crack between door and frame.

But this noisy night was different, for this grand storm outside my window also brought bursts of fire in its belly, and through the thin line at my bedroom door now danced great shocks of light, constant flashes of brilliance, blue and silver pulsing, pulsing without cease for minutes, hours, days, years. Declaring its place in the wildness of things.

This storm forced its way into my sleepy repose and dared me to look into its fire. So, I sat up and looked. And surprised I was to see the thin, dangerous fingers of glory. The glory of a violent sky, the brute beauty of heaven-fire pushed into my room through a thinness, and lying in the darkness before the brilliant light, it took me but a mere moment to understand that this tiny sliver of glory was all I could stand. Any more of it might have done me in. Ironically, my sightline to glory is thin, to hope to get a glimpse I must stay awake. I never considered that the fire of glory could be easy to miss, but now I know that one can sleep a life away and never see it, never be aware of its existence. Never search for it and therefore never find it.

And while I'm thinking about it, how have I lulled myself into believing that any of this is safe?

Was glory safe for Mary, for Joseph? For those simple shepherds just minding their business in the field at night? With what courage do mere mortals dare seek the glory of God?

The poet T.S. Eliot speaks to the profound nature of divine mystery, writing about being consumed by *fire.* I want to be consumed by fire and fire and fire – the brutal, fearful, dangerous, unpredictable fire of God's glory, 'tis a consummation devoutly to be wished.

And one worth staying awake for.

Watch and see, I tell the girls.

Diving for Pearls

I love teaching my English students to look for recurring, archetypal motifs and images in the literature we read together – I'm quite sure I have the best job in town.

Here's one. If the character stands outside during a rainstorm and gets drenched, it's most probably baptism imagery, and we can expect him to make a change, or at least try. Watch and see, I tell the girls, if the character doesn't come away from the soaking experience a changed person. And equally important, if he avoids the rain and runs back into his house dry as a bone, he's refusing the baptism and will probably grow more wretched as the story continues.

We learn to understand the imagery.

We also search for redemption or resurrection motifs. Here, a character must go down in order to come back up, he must stoop in order to lift. He finds himself down in the dust of his own choosing, often near death, but then he makes his decision to rise and live again, and he's a different person this time 'round. This is the lesson of literature – we must fall in order to rise. This is the story.

The Christmas story is no different. God descends in order

to reascend. He leaves behind the heights of glorious Heaven to become the tiniest of things, nestling deep down into the depths of the natural world – the darkness of a woman's womb. He comes down to come up again in order to bring the whole broken world along with Him. This is the story.

Think of a diver, stripped down to near-nakedness, diving headlong through the warm blue-green ocean water into the cold black depths, reaching into the dangers of hostile creatures and unexpected currents and rogue waves, reaching deep into the slime and decay of the ancient seabed, searching. For what is he searching? For what will he risk so much, invite such peril? Then up again from out of the deep, lungs almost bursting, the diver breaks into the light, triumphant, holding in his strong hand a tiny, dripping thing, the thing he risked his life to recover. A precious pearl that cost him a great price.

This is exactly the same story the angels sang about on that lonely Bethlehem night. I think my students would see this and understand.

So Many Stars!

The season of Advent reopens my mind to mystery. If one can explain a phenomenon, recreate it, validate the results in the lab, then that phenomenon is conclusive and no longer a mystery. Neither is it a miracle.

Based on the hypotheses of learned scientists who study the sky, one billion trillion stars exist in the observable universe. *One billion trillion*, who can fathom? The mass, the weight, the size of the idea alone flabbergasts such that I have to sit down in my chair and take a deep breath. So many stars! And all within the realm of human observation! Who among us dare dream what lies beyond the point the finest telescopes can reach?

If I dare to stand still in a lonesome field on a dark night and look up, if I take the time to go out there, the awful weight of mystery knocks me to my knees every time.

With the help of the theory of general relativity, scientists hypothesize that black holes exist. A black hole is a region of spacetime where gravity is so strong that nothing, including electromagnetic radiation, can escape it. Astronomers suggest that the black hole at the core of the elliptical galaxy Messier 87 has a mass about *seven billion* times that of the sun. Such fire! such heat! who is responsible? From where did all the mass come?

In what distant deeps or skies / Burnt the fire of thine eyes? shouts the poet William Blake during his day, standing at the mouth of his sybil cave of mystery.

A Virgin delivers a baby. That baby grows up to change water into wine, feeds thousands one afternoon with a couple of loaves of bread and a fish or two, and brings a young official's daughter back to life. Then He dies and brings Himself back to life. This is a mystery.

In this writer's opinion, the profound skepticism and anger of our post-modern age has led us far from mystery and delivered us soundly into the vast regions of distrust. Our imaginations now *fust in us unused*, as our brother Hamlet puts it, and in the place of imagination, we focus on self. Wonder shrivels and awe disappears; we grow satisfied with sanitized, linear conversations in language so guarded it dares to neither prick nor prod. It's exhausting, and worse, this idolization of self leaves no room at the inn of mystery.

The mystery of the Virgin birth disturbs many, as does the mystery of the Resurrection. As the mystery of the beauty and terror of an expanding, endless Universe disturbs me – I simply cannot grasp it. But this begs the question, why do we so readily accept some mysteries and so quickly scorn others?

Considering both mass and miracle, I wonder if scientists and theologians are in more accord than we imagine when it comes to matters of mystery – and maybe even miracle.

Waiting Rooms

Advent is a season about waiting, yet waiting is the very place where so many of us sink head-down and bottom-up right down into the slough of despair. Collectively as a culture, we hate waiting, we are bad at it. Perhaps this is because we view waiting as a passive state – things are out of our control and all that remains in our grubby paws is inactivity. Sitting, often alone, passively waiting it out.

Waiting for the doctor. Waiting for a text. Waiting for a court date. Waiting for a phone call. Waiting for COVID results. Waiting for a pregnancy test. Waiting for an answer. Waiting for a prodigal. Waiting for a birth. Waiting for a death. It can make one mad. We have even created physical rooms for all this waiting, for are we not always waiting for something?

But all this passivity does not exist in Advent, in the Christmas story. These characters are waiting in great anticipation for what's next; they seem to realize what we so often forget, that something brand-new has begun, and while the new thing is unknown and still gestating, it's coming nonetheless, whether we believe it or not. It is literally on its way.

What if, in the waiting rooms of our lives – and there are so many! – we could remember that something new is growing, that since nature abhors a vacuum, if something departs, a new wonder will eventually fill that void. And it is never what we expect.

What if we chose to live our moments in the wonder of anticipation rather than worry, or despair? That choice could change things. Those who choose to wait in active anticipation – Mary, Joseph, Zechariah, Elizabeth, you, me – are the rare few who choose to set aside all the useless, anxious fretting and live awake and present in the miracle of the moment – yes, even this very moment. I believe this is possible. I believe in us.

So, take heart and take charge! Most of what I wait for is completely out of my hands, but as I sit in my waiting rooms a'plenty, what remains in these empty hands of mine is hope.

The waiting room is the birthplace of hope.

TEARS

Turns out, tears are a part of this place. That's good news because everything makes me weepy these days. 'Tis the season, it seems, for tears. My grandson's first letter to Santa, written in bold SK letters, each letter a different size and color.

"Dear Santa, would you PLEASE bring me a lovie hippo? By Teddy. Thank you." Great letter, but I'm quite sure it was the "thank you" that brought the waterworks.

And kindness. Lord, the smallest acts of kindness – that sweet note from a student, generous rather than scornful words, rare glimpses of humility, any act of generosity – all these simply do me in these days.

Gentleness of any kind,
And all the grace that I can find,
A leaf, a twig, a bloom, a vine,
each gentle-nudges toward Divine.

A few weeks ago, my mother and I changed the arrangement on my father's grave. The indifferent summer sun had dyed the previous greenery into an obnoxious neon shade so overly-bright I could see the glowing from my parking space. So, my mother and I went to Michaels and bought several sprigs of holly with bright red berries and arranged it all into the small vase atop my father's marker stone. It wasn't the day itself that drove me deep into my Kleenex box – we actually laughed a lot, took pictures, told goofy stories – but rather the acknowledgment of another season passing, as seasons are so wont to do.

The poet Gerard Manley Hopkins rues the changing of life's seasons in this line I so love:

Margaret, are you grieving
Over Goldengrove unleaving?
Leaves like the things of man, you
With your fresh thoughts care for, can you?

The child Margaret weeps over the falling leaves, she loves the things of man, the lovely things of this life that are too beautiful and too precious to stay. But nothing gold can stay, the earth and the air and the things of man are always falling.

Perhaps it's the paradox of Advent that brings me most to tears. A baby is born to die, a child comes to save the world. One must be small to be great, poor to be rich, vulnerable to be powerful, last to be first, one must fall to rise. One must die to live. What kind of odd system is this?

The gospel message of Advent is so paradoxical it can turn heads toward disbelief or scorn or derision, or alas, even mockery. That is, until you stand by the grave of your beloved with winter flowers in hand and brush the fallen gold and orange and red leaves away from his beautiful name and finally see that the measure of what we can comprehend in no way limits the measure of God. Then paradox is the best news in town. It brings me to tears.

Mild He Lay His Glory By

Lately I've been writing about glory and shedding a few tears, and the waterworks aren't over yet and there's no end in sight. Do yourself a favor and do not sit beside me in school chapel these days. I cry through every hymn the schoolgirls sing, and oh my, how they've returned to singing in post-COVID-mitigated chapel. More robust singing as each day passes, it seems, and the more they sing, the more I weep. I leave chapel every day with a wetter mask than the day before. It's somehow like I'm hearing it all for the first time. Am I just now waking up? And if so, where have I been?

This week our assistant chaplain gave a chapel talk so full of truth the girls behind me were passing out tissues and wiping their noses on their sleeves. The speaker parsed out a lyric in one of the most familiar Christmas hymns, and I realized I'd never heard this before. Perhaps I really have been asleep, for a while.

Mild He lay His glory by, the young assistant chaplain sang to conclude her message.

> *Born that man no more may die,*
> *Born to raise the sons of Earth,*
> *Born to give them second birth.*
> *HARK! the herald angels sing*
> *Glory to the newborn King.*

Before He came here, Jesus enjoyed the full, infinite experience of being God. Glory. The perfection of Heaven. The actual presence of God crammed its enormous self into a person and came down here to help us. And to come here, to start to heal our broken world, He had to lay that glory by. He was willing, for us, to say goodbye to that giant, infinite, brilliant glory and come here, human-sized, and start to restore the world back to Eden, back to what it should have been before everything broke.

To help us, to heal us, He had to lay His glory by. Christ shows us how. By diminishing yourself, by de-glorifying yourself. Turns out this is the place of healing. In willing meekness, He lay His glory by. *He was meek and He was mild, He became a little Child*, the poet William Blake wrote through his own season of tears.

It doesn't make any sense, God laying His own glory by, God becoming man. But doesn't mystery defy sense, is that not its definition? Advent reminds us that the King of all Kings lay down his glory to become one of us, and what it looked like was a person who was mild.

What it means to be mild was the talk of the teacher's lunch table that afternoon, as it should be. And, of course, I wept.

Accustomed

In Fyodor Dostoevsky's *Crime and Punishment*, one of the notions that spurs much discussion among my bright AP scholars is the thematic line at the close of Chapter Two, that "man grows accustomed to everything, the scoundrel."

The protagonist Raskolnikov observes a noisy, drunken father interacting with his teenage daughter who has recently prostituted herself for the sake of the destitute family. Raskolnikov is disgusted by the man's inebriated display, proclaiming most philosophically the truth of human nature – we grow accustomed to things, good and bad, right and wrong, skewed or straight. Dostoevsky does not offer this idea as a comfort or a positive human quality, but rather as the norm. I concur but must then ask, what might "growing accustomed" look like?

As I see it, growing accustomed to the good things, the easy things, can lead to ingratitude, and quite quickly, I'm sad to report. And growing accustomed to bad things can leave us indifferent and lazy, apathetic to the hardships of others and overly accepting of the omnipresent malaise that plagues our generation. We harden ourselves to the thousands of things that "simply should not be" and stand before injustice and cruelty and our own sin and culpability and shrug our shoulders and refuse to be stirred.

Accustomed, we stand unmoved before the often-difficult stories of the world.

Perhaps this is where the story of Advent becomes most important. The experience of Advent is an awakening, a stirring, a shaking up. Everyone in the Christmas story was thoroughly shocked at this Birth – everyone – shepherds and kings and the pagan rulers of the day and unwed mothers and working-class fathers. The Christmas story demands that we move. We must do something with this story, face the sheer presumptuousness of it, and act upon it – accept or reject, but such an audacious tale demands more than indifference.

Only two roads diverge before us and we cannot travel both. Thus, we must choose to either energetically deny the miracle of the story and then embrace our denial with the unabashed fervor of a true skeptic and start preaching against it, or embrace the message with passion befitting the audacity of the story and get up off our La-Z-Boys and go help somebody!

The laziness we accept from ourselves in the name of logic, or the sheer ennui we embrace in simply growing accustomed to things is perhaps the greatest shock of all. No wonder the things of this world constantly shake us – it's God trying to wake us all up.

My Goodness

Everybody is a mess. Stumbling, fumbling around, trying to do good most of the time, I suppose. Trying to teach our children to be good, whatever that means. But trying to be good is a bit like skating on a frozen pond. Everybody is fine and happy and feels good about themselves as long as the ice remains predictable and secure. We try new moves and spins on the slick surface and challenge our fellow skaters to races and throw our arms up in the air at the glory of our own successes.

But what happens when the ice thins? When the power goes out and we are alone in the dark and in the cold? When our goodness, on which we've boasted and so relied, thins to the point of breaking? Things fall apart, the poet reminds us, and the center cannot hold. Goodness, as a virtue, can only take us so far. The ice eventually breaks – it will, it must.

The other December night a dutifully masked-up, ragtag threesome went to the Christmas concert at school – my mother, my daughter, and me, all together, bearing one another up for our first Christmas without Geezer. King Solomon said that a three-strand cord is not easily broken, so we three link arms like we always do, and go to the Mexican restaurant like we always do, and on to Christmas concert where we hear sung in sweet angelic harmony the same miraculous message that ragtag gathering at the manger heard, that gentle song the angels may have sung to the Virgin that night, reminding her – and all of us from then to now – that the Christmas story has absolutely nothing to do with the frailty of human goodness. Nay, this story is about the glorious saving power of love.

What Child is this, who, laid to rest
On Mary's lap is sleeping?
Whom angels greet with anthems sweet
While shepherds watch are keeping?

This, this is Christ the King
Whom shepherds guard and angels sing
Haste, haste to bring him laud
The babe, the son of Mary.

So bring Him incense, gold, and myrrh
Come, peasant, king, to own him
The King of kings salvation brings
Let loving hearts enthrone him.

That manger is as empty as the tomb, and in the place of goodness, which loses all meaning in these realms of human relativism, holy God offers salvation instead. So perhaps I should at least consider bringing Him a little laud, since I have neither incense nor proper intent nor myrrh nor money nor gold nor goodness-enough at hand, I will let my loving heart enthrone Him, I will try.

Thanks to goodness, everybody is a mess. But the tale told of Bethlehem's baby offers the antidote to goodness, which, of course, is very good news.

Ennui

The trappings of the Christmas season are, in a word, familiar. We drag live trees into our homes and light them in red and green, we demand stockings and tinsel and trim and mistletoe and chocolate-covered cherries and cards and selfies and posts and gifts and gifts and gifts. These things don't seem to change much, these expectations we place on ourselves and others to ensure the season is merry and bright. The demanding worldliness of such a season can grow tiresome, though, and oddly ironic as the story itself is about as other-worldly as it gets.

I have a question. Are we so convinced that the proper trappings, all the right stuff will make us happy that we have smothered the miraculous in familiarity? As if happiness were some submissive thing, firm and sure enough to house and handle our ever-growing list of demands and expectations.

It has been said that familiarity breeds contempt. Perhaps familiarity also breeds *ennui,* an indifference toward the sacred, a blasé attitude toward the miraculous.

Have I arrived at a place where beauty leaves me unmoved, where I am no longer flabbergasted at the wonder of a bird in flight or the miraculous face of a child? Am I too busy to stop for the first evening star on a cold night or to watch the fireball of our sun sink to darkness behind the flat horizon and weep at the glory of it?

Am I so busy with holiday home décor that I fail to see the terror in the eyes of the pregnant girl knocking at the door of my inn, and do I even wonder why I gave her a straw cot in my barn rather than my own bed? She's pregnant, for Heaven's sake, do I not care, have I gone blind?

Advent whispers the truth to those with ears to hear. In the cold silence of an ancient hillside, God visited earth, and his baby's night cry shattered Time and conquered Death. This is no myth, no recurring historical or literary motif, but rather something entirely new, a wonder so profound it defies language and borders the edges of fear.

There is nothing familiar or blasé about this story.

Casting Call for Annunciation

A Play in Three Acts

In another life, I directed high school theater, and I loved those days with all my heart. In my opinion and experience, high school theater is one of the best things on this earth; it's the gathering together of an odd, eclectic group of people with stories to tell in order to create the telling of another story about another odd, eclectic group. Glorious, magical, mysterious, and quite often, being in a show is the most fun you'll ever have.

Casting is key, though, to getting the thing right. A person cast in the wrong role weakens the whole show, there's no way around it, and enough miscast characters will doom a production. So, in order to properly cast a show, the director must really know and understand the storyline and the motivations of the characters. She must understand both the playwright's tone and intent – what the message of the play really is. Then and only then can she properly make the all-important cast decisions for the show.

During these busy days before the big day, as the eve of the event grows nearer, I'm ever eager to find a speck of time to consider, one more time, the oddest, quirkiest cast of characters ever assembled. Imagine this casting call, this particular cast of characters. Based on this cast list, one wonders and ponders the playwright's intention in writing this particular show in the first place.

Cast List/Dramatic Personae
(In order of appearance):

ANGEL, named Gabriel: Sent from God, actor must be large in frame with a deep, resounding voice

ELIZABETH: Woman, well advanced in years, becomes pregnant in her old age

ZECHARIAH: Mute man, husband of the pregnant Elizabeth (see above)

MARY: Pregnant teen, female, unmarried, probably small in stature, eager face

JOSEPH: Carpenter, working-class male, engaged to Mary (see above), devoted

HEROD and SCRIBES: Older men, agitated, political sorts, buffoonish, not caricatures, but almost

SHEPHERDS: Bedraggled workers of a lower class, all male, preferably heavily bearded

MAGI: Astrologers, men of Asian descent, royal in stature

CHORUS: Angels on high, strong singing voices required

BABY: Named Jesus, newborn, average-looking

Director's Note: With sixty-six total books in the series, this multi-ethnic, multi-generational, cross-cultural story has staying power. This is a large-hearted cast of characters, all acquainted with exile, crying for blessing and salvation but ever full of promise and ignited by hope. An eager group who refuses to remain silent about what they have seen. Well, most of them.

Here's what the cast and crew need to know, the playwright's message in a nutshell, the importance of this play ANNUNCIATION. It is vital that the cast understand this intent in order to accurately portray for the audience the importance and immediacy of the message. This Annunciation, this announcement, heralds a complete change in the order and thought of all earthly things. Just beyond the horizon lie eternal truths, realities, and the announcement of these things, the glorious whispers of their song, can be heard on the sunrise, if one is quiet, if one is listening.

The villains in the story will neither hear nor believe, for they are too noisy with their own shouting and closed ears and the naysaying they love so well to listen to any message but their own, lovers of their own voices are they. But the quiet and humble characters will hear the announcement, and they will believe. The main event may be far off still, but it is coming, for it has been announced. Just wait, just watch, you'll see.

Tomorrow, when the curtain rises, we shall know and be glad.

I'd like to know what actually happened.

Obliquity

I just finished reading Steinbeck's *East of Eden* with my young English scholars, several of whom stay back after class most days to talk about choice, the novel's primary thematic idea. And, as per the book's title, we talk a great deal about Eden.

I have questions about the origin of things, don't you? So many questions about Eden. I'd like to know what actually happened to the physical earth when the Edenic pair ate the fruit forbidden – did the earth itself feel the shift when Paradise was suddenly lost? Was there an earthquake as perfection slipped out of balance or was it just a simple shiver, the first primordial shudders in the tectonic plates? And what about the animals? Did the animals of the garden groan, howl in despair at the earth's loss of innocence, could they feel the difference or did they simply continue to graze without a care in the lush Edenic green?

Perhaps this Fall from perfection was so jarring to the whole of creation that Earth actually tilted 23.4 degrees on its axis into its current state of obliquity. Think of that.

Or perhaps the Fall was a slow thing, like a poison easing its steady way into the whole system, intoxicating the first gardeners initially with shame – the very first negative feeling – when their eyes were opened and they realized their nakedness. And then intoxicating them further with blame – the very first negative action – which inevitably followed. Whatever happened, Creation took us and shook us. Adam and Eve fell, and their hearts turned away from God – this is our inheritance.

But there's more, there's always more. When the earth shook and shifted, God did not. When the earth shakes and shifts, God does not. Faith is a rock, the unshakeable rock on which to lean as the world around us quivers and quakes, and make no mistake, shake it will. Things around here have been shaky since the start.

But nonetheless, steadfastness abounds. Steadfastness is not a mere personality trait of the lucky, it's a choice. A steadfast person chooses to stand on the Rock – or hide in its shadow – steady in the midst of the ever-present, inevitable shaking.

Advent reminds us that we are not alone here. God has never left us alone, never forsaken us, and to prove it, He lay his own glory aside and squeezed Himself into the form of a tiny baby and lived among us. Then died, then lived again.

Dang. That's a story even Steinbeck couldn't pen.

EARTHRISE

I came across a photograph of the Earthrise that stopped me in my tracks. Earthrise is the rising of the bright blue earth above the horizon of the bleak, dusty lunar horizon. And to think, two regular guys named Neil and Buzz actually saw this sight, can you imagine? They just stood there on the moon and with their own two regular eyes looked at their planet, their earth rising above the horizon of the moon. I wonder if, off camera, those guys fell down into the moondust in sheer awe, or perhaps terror, gazing upon the lonely beauty of their home, that enormous blue-lit ball so very far away.

Do you know what's missing from that iconic photo? Go take a look. Stars. There are virtually no stars in that black sky of the photograph. The bright light of the earth, this glorious reflector of the sun, is simply too bright for the naked eye to see the myriad movement of the stars and galaxies surrounding and the heavens beyond. The glorious blue light of earth is all we can see, everything else fades to darkness.

In the same way, let your light shine before others that they may see your good deeds and glorify your Father in heaven. But what does *this* earthly light look like? Is this mere metaphor? What inexplicable brute beauty am I supposed to shine so that others can see?

Faith, steadfastness even when mocked, faithful in the face of scorn.

Hope, against the ever-rising tide of despair, which, by the way, is not new to this old blue world of ours.

And Love, without the demand of reciprocity, without any demands at all. Love, the very opposite of scorn – a simple act of justice, kindness for kindness' sake without the need to post to Insta, patience with a child, patience with anyone. Love, which bears all things, believes all things, hopes all things, endures all things.

People who live like this – or try to, or have the desire to, or believe it's even possible, or try again after failing, or forgive regardless of the circumstances, or return kindness in place of cruelty, or hold fast to hope – these humble folk are beacons on a hill, lights so bright in the deep darkness that even beauty pales in their presence. This light we all can see. It awakens, intimidates, and even terrifies. But in all its lonely grandeur, this light alone shines brightest.

You are the light of the world, a city set on a hill, a lamp on a stand. This is the message, the reason for Advent in the first place.

Most Favored One

If we can understand a thing, then it's no longer a mystery. Let's consider for a moment Mary's point of view. Barely old enough to conceive, Mary is visited by the angel Gabriel who greets her with a new name, "Most Favored One."

What might Mary be thinking? What was it like to sit before divine glory and ultimate mystery and hear the miraculous message designed for no other but her, what was it like to be the chosen one?

The sheer amount of human art and literature alone surrounding the Virgin Birth of Christ finds the topic worthy of consideration.

What might Mary be thinking?

Take a look for a moment at the Virgin Mary in Henry Ossawa Tanner's *The Annunciation.* I cannot stop looking at her face. How alone she looks, but not afraid. How intently she listens to the message of the angel – the angel of the Lord – and, rather than losing her voice, she somehow finds it: *How can this be?* her only question, her only question!

Or Botticelli's peaceful Mary, bowing her head.

Or Fra Lippo Lippi's Mary, with her eyes closed as the angel Gabriel tells her the news.

Or the Dutchman Gerard David's Mary, arms crossed, clad in Dutch blue robes, kneeling before her book – that face, that awestricken face. Is she worried? What must she be thinking?

This moment reminds me anew of T.S. Eliot's notion of the still point and that only at the still-point is there dance, and Brennan Manning's observations on the same, how the shipwrecked stand at the same still-point of a turning world and discover that the human heart is made for Christ and cannot really be content with less.

All this pitch and thought, all but a few mere moments before the power of the Most High overshadows Mary and the whole of human history is changed. Forevermore, amen.

How can this be? People can shrug off the miracle of the Virgin Birth all they want, for without miracle or mystery, Jesus' birth is merely human, just like all the other regular babies born before and after, birthed from a young woman who simply refuses to tell the truth of his paternity.

If we can understand a thing, it's not a miracle, and we are already wont to explain things away. The miraculous requires the work of a living God, and His Son, who was indeed no regular child.

The Still Point

I've been thinking about movement lately and how the Christmas story demands we move, get up off our rumps, and do something rather than merely wallowing in all the grit and grime with which we have grown so accustomed. And I stand by those words.

But we mere mortals need balance too, lest we stray too far off course, and the necessary balance for all the movement in this turning world is, of course, stillness – we are called to both.

Mary is not alone in Bethlehem's birth story, you know. This miraculous Birth is not limited to a tiny stable in ancient Israel. No, no, this Birth, if it matters at all, is for the whole world. This Birth must take place within me as well, and the mystery will be brought forth only in stillness.

I ponder this idea and wonder, what is this still point? Is a quieting of spirit enough? Perhaps moving toward stillness is more than mere quiet. Perhaps moving toward stillness is indeed movement, the active process of laying-down the passions and opinions that so easily beset and entrap me, imprison me rather than set me free.

One mystic said that human nature is like a stable inhabited by the ox of passion and the ass of prejudice. Do these beasts remain in my stable, I ask myself, pretending to be shocked, but at the still point of my turning world I know these beasts stand strong in my stable because I feed them on the quiet, in the darkness of night where I fancy my indulgences hidden. But the Birth. The Birth in my soul can drive beasts to their knees. The Birth in my soul sparks the flame of faith I inherited at my own birth. The Birth whispers to me, stirs in me hope that the intimacy with God lost in the Garden is not lost at all, but rather, ready to be found again – regained, restored, reborn! But where? Where is it?

At the still point. It is alone at the still point the morning wren sings her loveliest, albeit most heart-wrenching song. But alas, she stands at her still point, and soon she shall dance.

SPRING

2020

Lent is upon me before I realize that March is Women's History Month. Does recent history count? 2020 was a doozy of a year, one for the books indeed, full of story and suspense and work and change and a new appreciation for the unknown and uncharted.

Here's what one woman's 2020 looked like, my mother's recent history.

In one calendar year, the year of our Lord 2020, my mother packed up sixty-two years of marriage and put their house on the market. She decided which stuff would make the big move and which would not, and there was *a lot of stuff.* Hint: take as little as possible, the freedom is in the release of the stuff.

Sold a car.

Managed an estate sale (again, too much stuff).

Relocated to a wonderful retirement community, managed the move herself, made many decisions (my father's dementia prohibited any decision-making on his part), settled in, made new friends.

Cared remotely for my father in the nursing facility. Kept Geezer and most of the nursing staff well-stocked in homemade cookies and brownies and Pancho's cheese dip and chips.

Pre-grieved.

Kept up with and cared for her friends and allowed her friends to care for her as my father's health worsened by the day.

Had her hip replaced.

Turned eighty-years old.

Pre-grieved.

Interviewed and hired extra help for my father during COVID.

Called my brother and me when she needed help.

Followed the slow ambulance to the hospital.

Pre-grieved.

Stayed bedside with Geezer for eleven days and nights, sleeping on the vinyl couch in the hospital room.

Closed on her house the day before Geezer died, sitting in the front seat of the car of a most lovely and compassionate closing attorney who met her in the hospital parking lot in the winter cold-and-sleet so my mother wouldn't have to leave the hospital and drive in the bad weather to close on her house.

Held my father's hand as he passed.

Planned a funeral.

Grieved.

2020 was an historic year for my mother, exhausting in every way. Yet, the other day I asked my mother how she was doing and without a pause she replied, You know, I think I'm good. I'm not jealous of anyone else's life, I'm content right where I am. I'm happy with the decisions I've made.

I'm not jealous of anyone else's life, she said. Now you know why I want to be like my mother when I grow up.

This is my tiny contribution to Women's History Month.

SUMMIT

Heraclitus states that no man ever steps in the same river twice, for it is not the same river and he is not the same man. I say this must also be true of a stepping back onto a great smoky mountain.

Last spring, my husband and I hiked to the summit of Mount LeConte, the highest peak completely in the state of Tennessee. There exist many paths to the summit, but we chose the Alum Cave Trail, eleven miles round trip. The trail notes say the hike to the top, while not technically challenging, is strenuous. I concur.

We had hiked this peak once before, a bit over twenty years ago, but we are different hikers now. The joys and hardships and losses and gains of a decade or two change a person, change a couple for better and for worse. In my memory, those younger hikers – we, then – were in a hurry, such a big hurry, for there was much to do and still so much to prove in that day; exactly what, I now can't seem to remember, but it all seemed so important then.

We brought no supplies that day all those years back, not a power bar or an apple or even water, for our plan was to hike only the 2.2 miles up to Alum Bluff Cave, take a look around, and then head back down. We'd eaten pancakes and bacon at the

Pancake Pantry that morning, fuel enough for a short hike, but after resting a moment at the Alum Bluff Cave – which is in fact a concave bluff about eighty feet in height – we saw the wooden trail marker for Mount LeConte and decided on a whim to climb to the summit and never thought a thing about it. And, for the record, we made it up the mountain just fine, jogging up portions of the trail, unencumbered by the gear and tackle and trim others deem essential – we liked to brag about that. I did succumb, though, at the summit and asked an experienced hiker if she might kindly share one of her bananas for two lunatics who summited the mountain unprepared, with nothing in hand – alas, even pancakes go only so far. The generous woman smiled and gave us two.

This time, though, we older hikers are more prepared. My husband totes water and bananas and granola bars and raisins in his backpack, and I find a sturdy walking stick about half-way up. We care less about the bragging now, at least I fancy we do. Making it safely through the day without injuring self or others proves to be goal enough.

The bottom third of the trail is easy, warm and wide. Wooden bridges cart us over the fast-moving creek again and again; I dearly love this water that sings the song of my childhood. We trek through Arch Rock and keep on moving up, up, steady and slow.

At Alum Bluff Cave the trail turns steep and stays that way. We older hikers grow quiet and focus on our footing, acknowledging now what we had no time for all those years ago, that both beauty and danger await the traveler; such is the wild way of the trail. The white trillium is in full bloom this day, perfuming the path, alongside the Solomon's seal with its tiny, white bell-shaped blossoms, and the rosebay rhododendron, the great mountain laurel that will choke the trail in early summer blooms now nods her welcome in tiny hints of white and pink blossom.

We pause for water. We care to take a look.

Close to the top, the air grows much colder, the ledges and creek beds and wooden stairsteps still quite slick from winter's icy touch. We pay attention to our footfalls. The forest itself grows unexpectedly thick near the top, its green canopy darkening the path; yet the dense mosses shine with smooth easy green in the afternoon sun, and just like in Moses' day on his mountain, water literally springs from the cracks and crags of the rocks.

We meet fellow hikers coming down from the heights, all reporting the same message like a great crowd of witnesses who have gone before us: stay strong and watch your step, you are mere minutes from the summit, this last bit is the hardest but the trek is worth all the effort you've got, the work is part of the reward. One foot in front of the other.

Finally, after three hours or so, the heavy forest breaks and we weary hikers find ourselves at the rocky top of Mount LeConte. Here, on the small, rough top of the world, the mountains and the sky are one, and the air itself is blue and blue and fills the eternal sky with blue, and the ancient mountains are blue and silent, and we mortals hover now on the fragile edges of sheer cliffs in this sacred thin place, high and lifted up, above even the birdsong.

I do not remember this blue air and these blue mountains. I cannot recall ever seeing this infinite sky. Is it possible I've been here before, is it possible I've forgotten this wonder, is it possible my younger self missed this glory, too busy begging a banana and snapping a selfie?

Soon enough, the sun heads west and there is a time for every season under heaven and it is our time to descend. One cannot remain in glory, not on earth anyway. We take one last look then turn away toward home.

Our younger selves pass us, a noisy group of laughing twenty-somethings jogging (jogging!) past us on their way down from the heights. I speak to them as they pass, recommending short, cautious steps and also a stop at Inspiration Point where one can get a glimpse of the Eye of the Needle near the top of Little Duck Hawk Ridge.

But I do not think they hear me.

THE COMMUNITY OF THE BROKEN

The girl in the elevator at the Bass Pro Shop in Memphis said to be sure to get the fudge. It's famous, she says. But not today because we are out of fudge today, she says. So, I am standing in line at the fudge store to buy my father some sugared-pecans and a Diet Coke instead when a cool hand gently touches my warm one in recognition. I turn to look into eyes I do not know, an older gentleman with a lovely silver-haired woman by his side, but somehow his touch is completely familiar.

It is a touch I have felt all my life. We have something in common, he says before he introduces himself. Indeed, we do.

The kindly stranger takes my three-fingered hand into his own fingerless palm and pats my hand warmly with his other hand, his *good hand,* an overly intimate gesture in almost every other circumstance imaginable, movement far too fast and familiar for strangers, but we are not strangers. We are members of the same community.

We stand together in the fudge-less fudge line and talk of background – he's from England – and education – I'm a teacher. And spouses – ours stand beside us smiling and nodding knowingly at each other. Between them they have watched these interactions, these immediate friendships bloom year after year. The older man and I talk well past the time everyone else is ready to go. The pecans and Diet Coke arrive as does his popcorn and coffee, so it is time for me to step out of line and take my father his snack; I figure he's also ready to go visit the vast selection of the fishing rods and reels. My new friend and his wife are going to look at the boats.

It was so nice to meet you, I say. Always is. You are beautiful, he says, patting my hand one last time. You are too. We wave our *little hands* at each other in parting solidarity. Our spouses grin and wink, not a one of us new to this stage.

I was born into the community of the broken, a unique place of loveliness in the universe. Humility dwells there, as does compassion and kindness; empathy is birthed in the fertile ground of this company. This is an enviable lot in which to toss one's hat. It is not hard to be a vital part of the community of the broken; one must only admit her brokenness. Something slightly easier to do when you are born that way, I think. I was born with a limb difference, this is what the kids are calling it these days. *Symbrachydactyly* is its proper name.

My brokenness is physical, visible for all the world to see. The great and unexpected blessing in the visibility of one's brokenness is that there is no denying it, no hiding. Other broken-folk, like my friend in the fudge line, can see my brokenness and come forth with theirs, if they choose. On crutches and in wheelchairs, limb-differed and limbless, the mentally-challenged and the sick, I can *see* your brokenness and you can see mine.

And the Lord said, It is good. Here I am, world, as I am. Take it or leave it is surely the battle cry of the broken, a beautiful, liberating anthem.

So, when a member of this community approaches me in line and takes my little hand into his, it's a touch with which I am familiar, an ancient kinship, something much more than mere compassion. It is the humble touch of understanding. Our love is deep before we ever even speak. He gets me.

It's harder, I've found, with *invisible brokenness.* No one can see our hidden things, and we've all been experts at hiding since the dawn of man.

Adam, where are you?

This broken community is harder to find because of its invisibility. Sadnesses and failures, despair and distrust, wounds old and un-mended make up the universal fabric of human brokenness, and yet we all camouflage and deny and pretend it isn't happening to us; we hide our hurts behind smiles and lies and odd, heavy clothing, and in the worst-case scenarios, we try to protect our own hidden broken places by exposing the brokenness in others. Judgment and prejudice and gossip are perfect garments to cower behind, for pointing out the ills in others just *may* buy one a little bit more time and space to dig her own hiding holes a little bit deeper.

Whew, it's exhausting.

When I was a teenager, I didn't like walking on the beach in the summer. The beach, where pretty girls strut and fret their hours walking to and fro with good-looking guys following an acceptable distance behind, everyone watching, everyone hoping. I didn't mind the walking when my right arm was beachside and my little arm was oceanside, but when we turned to walk back, it was harder. Do you know this feeling?

It is the fragility of exposure, a very hard place. The community of the broken can help to heal this place. Honest brokenness strengthens the fragile and emboldens the weak. Gentle, healing grace, where the broken are made whole again.

Christ's brother James tells us to confess our sin, our broken places, and to pray for one another, so that we may be healed. *I'll show you mine and you can show me yours because it's all the same.* We are all the same because we all need the same healing. The beautiful community of the broken is comprised of people with gracious ears who see and hear our stories of pain and loss and respond not with judgment but with understanding and empathy deep. Folk who take your hand – physically, emotionally, spiritually – and say, I understand your loss and sadness and pain because mine is the same. We are the same, all cut from the same tragically-flawed but intricately-designed human cloth. This community is comprised of people who walk hand-in-hand with you down the beach and, rather than trying to hide their stuff, they get t-shirts instead. *Ten fingers are overrated* the little girl's tee-shirt proudly confesses, the little girl with *symbrachydactyly*, same as me. No hiding here.

What would your t-shirt say?

This is the beginning of healing – the confession of broken places. *This* is a better way of living, praying for each other so that we may be healed. I happily and humbly join and rejoin the throngs of the broken for as long as we all shall live.

I see my fudge-line friend again before I leave Bass Pro. He's holding an ice cream cone in his good hand and waving maniacally with his little fingerless one. I wave back with my little hand and shout across duck-laden ponds, It was so great to meet you, have a safe trip!

You too, dearest, his British accent wafts lightly over the country music. So much love to you.

He means it. I receive his healing.

But the table laughs and the mountain smiles and the wine flows.

ON WRITING IN GOOD COMPANY

In the mountains of North Carolina
laughter slips through pine branches toward the water
and the mountain sings her pink refrain, joined
by the blue treble notes of wood sparrows.

It is the last evening, and I have seen how
a sowing collective outweighs a sowing singular,
and I remember that
sowing is a good, fine thing.

Flax heaped on flax and wheat on wheat
is abundance in its time,
but who among the hungry considers the fingers of the sowers,
fingers inked and nails gnawed.

When bounty comes
who first considers the planting, or the sweat?
Perhaps their own mothers do not understand
the toil such birthing requires.

But the table laughs and the mountain smiles and the wine flows
and letters become a child's first words
and phrases begin to bear the heft of memory
and the creek carries the song toward center
as it always has
in faith, which after all is the substance of things hoped for.

Perhaps the wine alone knows the sowing,
the crushing,
for wine understands that brokenness is sweetest
in the company of the broken.

Dancing Over Thresholds

The door creaks open and in they come, an eclectic assortment of sympathetic souls. Mid-week tired, slow, winter-cold or summer-hot, they shuffle over our threshold on Wednesday nights and sit in straight-backed chairs, no longer enough overstuffed chairs for all who come. My heart leaps up as they begin to settle, and I slow to watch, I quiet to hear, and I sit among them in the wonder of this assembly.

My, what an odd lot we are.

A bunch of broken scarecrows scratching around, finding seats, cozying up on the couch, too many folk, too little couch, all of us doing what people do – getting coffee, eating one of those butterscotch cookies Allen bakes every week, fetching water, petting the dog. On the lookout for a little more peace and a little more grace, we come mid-week to open Scripture, to seek, hopefully to find something along the way. My eyes quick-fill with the unexpected grace of it all. It surprises me every time.

Crossing a threshold is an important thing; a hopeful vulnerability dwells at that thin strip that separates one place from the next. A weighty place, a threshold, a place to remove a mask if I can remember to try, to lay aside the face I've prepared to meet the other faces I meet. Folk ease in and smile their gentle smiles, and I smile mine. People like me, afraid to be fully known but with a great longing for just that, and a deep desire to be forgiven, and loved.

My, what an odd, needy lot we are.

My friend sits beside me, my friend who lost her baby, only days old, to a heart defect, a broken heart. Oh, the weight of such sadness, such despair. All words pale beside such grief. Yet my friend comes and sits and prays and waits, expectantly. Yes, she expects again, with fear and caution, but she expects, her belly once again firm and filling. We expect with her and sit with her and pray together. What else can we do?

The bringer of cookies just lost his brother. He bakes as he heals, it seems, slow and steady. He crosses this threshold with hands full and crosses back with heart full; I suppose it's a pretty good trade-off, week after week – there's hope enough in it. One friend is in constant pain in her back, one has arthritis in her knees and can't play tennis any more. One of us has lost her voice and the doctors can't seem to figure out why; she goes back to doctor soon to see what's to be done and wants us to pray for her.

Another friend has never been able to have children. The other week, at the last minute, our regular church nursery worker couldn't come, and I was looking for quick help and ran right into my friend in the hallway outside the nursery. I could use your help, I say. I'd do anything for you, she smiles. Could you watch the littlest ones today? I ask. Long pause.

I never had any kids, you know, I'm not sure how to do it, she says. Yet she did it anyway, for love, and the littlest ones ran and clung to her, smiled and loved her, kissed her with the wettest of sticky-kisses, as if to say Where have you been? We've been waiting for you. And tonight, at the mid-week gathering, she speaks of this newfound delight with a happy lilt and gives a soft praise for a most unexpected gift, a new joy, unforeseen – the love of children.

They loved me, she said, and all I did was say *yes.*

The girl with the long flowing curls has been gone from us for a long time, at MD Anderson. One of those one-in-a-million chance tumors, a big one, creeping into her eye. Bone from her leg to repair her palette, some teeth now missing. Slow-to-walk, slow-to-talk. We prayed for her hard, so hard, and tonight she walks slowly back to us, soft-steps over this threshold. Texas cannot have her, she's ours.

Another of us is filled with joy this night, celebrating eleven years of sobriety. We clap our hands and smack his back and eat more cookies.

My, what a beautiful, odd lot we are.

What a privilege to count myself among them, this curious, sacred company. A peculiar people. All of us tip-toeing carefully through our pain, hand on the shoulder of another who has felt similar stings. It's a curiously choreographed dance, a love-filled frenzied ballet *en pointe,* a delicate search for balance. In a *pas de trois*, the dancers move together in symmetry through much of the dance, but also attempt a variation alone, a solo. The *pas de trois* concludes with a *coda*, a finale usually set to music of a quick tempo in which the dancers bring the piece to a spectacular finish.

This is what we do.

We come together on Wednesday evenings to learn to move with a bit more ease, a bit more symmetry, to help each other prepare for the certain difficult solos that come. Our collective movement is sometimes beautiful, elegant even, but mostly we creep, limp, slouch toward grace, waving hopeful hands at joy and joy and joy-to-come. We are here to help each other toward a more spectacular finish, and in that pursuit, there are flashes of joy here tonight, dancing above the cookies, great splashes of love.

One of us has been sick, stumbling and falling, and hasn't been here for a while, but tonight she comes, holding tight to an arm as she threshold-crosses. She settles snugly in the brown leather chair we save for her by the fireplace, and I bring her coffee – don't get up, please don't fall again. She is a quiet, rarely speaking any more but ever listening, coffee sipping.

We are all here, so we begin.

Our sacred few mid-week moments commence with words of praise, thanksgiving, efforts at gratitude for the things in our lives, even the hard things, communal encouragement. Beauty in the spoken word, let us encourage the brethren. Who has something she is grateful for, something that will encourage us as we begin? Where have you seen God at work in these days? Sometimes a hard question for broken folk.

Tonight, it is quiet. No words yet, just a settling in, breaths deep. It seems to have been a trying week.

The coffee-drinker in the leather chair moves, scoots forward. She has been so ill and gone from us so long. The quietest of us, the hardest to hear, we are unaccustomed to her voice. She opens her mouth to try to offer words of praise, to speak. But instead, this night, she surprises us, surprises herself.

She begins to sing.

Praise God from Whom all blessings flow… Her scratchy, throaty voice fills, lifts up to the ceiling beams, so unexpected to us and to her, elegant, ethereal. A sudden song of stunning praise, unrehearsed, like hearing a miracle.

Praise Him all creatures here below... One by one, we reverently join her song, we creatures here below, trying to praise Him in this astonishing moment, doing our best, throwing tattered rags of praise at holy feet.

Praise Him above, ye heavenly host... Are they singing with us, even now, the heavenly hosts? Shhhhhh, do I actually hear their heaven-voices echoing in my den? Are the birds and trees joining in? I think perhaps they are.

Praise Father, Son, and Holy Ghost. Amen and amen.

There are as many different pitches as singers in this road-weary, mid-week, world-worn choir – high notes too high, low notes too low. Yet voices and tears mingle here and we hear a fresh harmony in the ancient song. I've never done anything like that before, the impromptu singer marvels as we wipe our tears.

Isn't that what a miracle is, something inexplicable, never done before? The wondrous miracle of praise, a sacrifice. I can hear notes still ringing in the high rafters of my den, the birds warbling the tune this morning as I write.

The sacrifice of praise is everyone's song.

In her essay "An Expedition to the Pole," Annie Dillard reads from the solemn and stolid diaries of early Artic explorers. With almost his dying breath, Swedish explorer Salomon Andree writes, Our provisions must soon and richly be supplemented, if we are to have any prospect of being able to hold on for a time.

That's it. We live on Artic ice floes, drifting, hard-stuck in the ice, under-provisioned. If we have any hope of being able to hold on, we must supplement our stock and store, bring in fresh supplies, replenish with regularity. Who survives long, alone on a cold, lonely island?

Our mid-week hour is short. Too soon comes the time to dance back over the threshold into the world, but these dancers and singers are slow departers. Can't we just stay here? This togetherness works for us, and I am melancholy to dim the last lights. The beauty of the *pas de trois* is that it is danced together, each helping the other to achieve greatness, a spectacular finish.

Together we dance our broken, crooked, beautiful, scarecrow ballet, and God says It is good. I becomes we, us. So let us go forth in joy, to love and serve the Lord. And ah, let us dance.

Almost Bloomed

In the early spring, the path of our daily walk is filled with flowers not yet open, waiting in patient silence for the moment of their blooming. Today I see the almost-opened daffodil, her tight knot of petals stretching at their seams. Standing on the threshold of grandeur, the cluster of almost-bloomed daffodils dance to and fro in the warming breezes, waving their weedy green fingers at the future, which is the definition of hope. Content to wait, they neither toil nor spin, they are neither sad nor lonely.

If, and only if, I lean all the way down to the ground and bend my stubborn knees to the dirt and angle my ear to the hard and holy ground, only then might I whisper my heart-deep question, What are you waiting for? If I hone my stubborn ears to hear Nature's whispers, if I wield them into momentary submission, then I sometimes hear the whispered tune of the earth, the flowers' easy song. We are waiting for the Gardener, the One who can be trusted.

The flower-almost-bloomed seems to understand that deferring to a timetable larger than herself is not failure, but faith. And as she waits, she dances in the fluttering springtime breezes.

Hope is often deferred, but when it is fulfilled, it is a bed of golden daffodils.

ALMOST CONTENT

Memphis' water supply system suffered in the unusual snow storms of February 2021. Broken pipes and disturbed water mains such that those-in-charge placed the city under a "boil water advisory."

For about a week, we, the fine citizenry of the Bluff City, had to boil our own drinking water, and this straw broke the back of a friend of mine.

NOW WE HAVE TO BOIL OUR OWN WATER! she cried in her February discontent. After all the disruptions of 2020 – strained elections and COVID-19 and quarantine and fires and civil unrest in the streets – it was the drinking water that did her in. Boiling her own water was the breaking point, and she was simply too tired to do it.

IT'S LIKE WE LIVE IN A THIRD WORLD COUNTRY! she anguished. Actually, no. Is this water potable? is a question much of the world wonders every day but rarely-if-ever in Memphis, Tennessee. The good folk at Memphis Light, Gas, and Water got our clean water back within a week. Thanks be to God.

Two roads diverged in a yellow wood, the poet wrote. Could we imagine for a moment the two divergent roads from which we must choose are contentment and discontent?

Is it too bold of me to posit that contentment, at least in part, is a choice? The choice is not whether I will boil the water; boiling water I must. The choice is the how I approach that which I cannot avoid, my attitude toward the inevitable.

Is it too bold of me to suggest that our ability to choose contentment is greater than choosing happiness?

I search my photo library for a picture to accompany these thoughts. Nature, as a whole, seems content with its particular situation, so I chose a kid instead. A sweaty, happy kid sitting on the counter eating cookie dough, my grandson, face and hands covered in dough, mixer beater stuffed in his mouth. What this kid doesn't know yet is that soon he will have to make a choice after another kid on the playground says he doesn't want to play with him anymore. My grandson will then have to find a new friend, he will have to choose contentment in another space.

But it happened, of course. A kid on the playground didn't want to play with my grandson and he *did* have to find a new friend. And he did it, and now the two are as thick as peanut butter and jelly, happily climbing on the monkey bars and playing swords with sticks.

If I believe that contentment is a choice – and I do believe that – then why do I choose to live far too much of my life hanging out on the far rims of contentment?

Fyodor Dostoevsky (1821-1881)

From The Brothers Karamazov

"... active love is a harsh and fearful thing compared with the love in dreams. Love in dreams thirsts for immediate action, quickly performed, and with everyone watching. Indeed, it will go as far as the giving even of one's life, provided it does not take long but is soon over, as on stage, and everyone is looking on and praising. Whereas active love is labor and persistence, and for some people, perhaps, a whole science."

Almost Love

In this short life, there are only two things worth our time or any merit – loving God and loving our neighbors.

But the practicality of this matter is slippery, for I *want* to love my neighbor, and I *almost* love my neighbor. I mean, I like most people, except the irritating ones. I don't like the irritating ones because they are unlikeable – all those democrats and republicans and liberals and conservatives and vaxed and unvaxed and needy and Christian and Muslim and Jewish and and and and and and . . .

I love the idea of loving my neighbor, I even encounter the nightly dream of loving the whole world. But the truth is the world is crass and undignified and selfish and noisy and all of that is hard to love.

Yet, I have come to believe in active love that is one-directional. A love where reciprocity is *not* a prerequisite. This kind of love says, My neighbor will not reach out to me, so I will reach out to her. This kind of love is my friend Leigh getting out on a cold, rainy December night and driving to a far-off, difficult neighborhood to help a desperate young woman make something better of herself, even if the young woman cannot reciprocate the love because she doesn't yet know how. In fact, active love neither demands reciprocity nor looks for it. Expecting to be compensated for a loving act is something other than love; duty perhaps, some form of legalism, something with far less grace – a kind of almost-love.

If I'm fussy because I didn't receive a proper thank-you for the good deed I performed, then a good deed was all I accomplished – a civilized gesture certainly, yes, but not love. Almost-love.

A colleague of mine once said, in a moment of great annoyance, I will no longer tolerate the intolerant. I appreciate the word-play, but nowhere in this is love.

Love costs, it's active. Active love means forgiving first. A movie in the 70's said, Love means never having to say you're sorry. Alas, active love means just the opposite. Dreams of love are mere shadows, talk of action without love is sounding brass and tinkling cymbals. But, as a single ray of sun light warms tender green shoots into new growth, so it goes with active love. We know it when we see it. We feel it when we receive it. We understand it when we practice it.

We are most like God when we are freely pursuing another person's love, giving the grace we desire. Everything else is imagination, mere love in dreams.

Gerard Manley Hopkins (1844-1899)

Pied Beauty

Glory be to God for dappled things—
  For skies of couple-colour as a brinded cow;
    For rose-moles all in stipple upon trout that swim;
Fresh-firecoal chestnut-falls; finches' wings;
  Landscape plotted and pieced—fold, fallow, and plough;
    And all trades, their gear and tackle and trim.
All things counter, original, spare, strange;
  Whatever is fickle, freckled (who knows how?)
    With swift, slow; sweet, sour; adazzle, dim;
He fathers-forth whose beauty is past change:
                Praise Him.

Almost Perfect

Glory be to God for dappled things –

The poet Gerard Manley Hopkins writes this, one of my favorite lines in all of poetry, and this spring morning his imperfect words bring me home.

Glory be to God for dappled things –

The landscape plotted and pieced, the simple leaves awake again in their glorious dappled shades and shapes, not one the same as another. The snowflakes falling in Memphis, this unusually cold wintry freeze in the land of the Delta blues, and every single one of them different – original, spare, strange.

Glory be to God for dappled things –

As pure as the shocking blue of a cloudless sky is, surely the dappled sky more glorious; cloud-filled and unpredictable in its mystery. I am ever shocked at the endless variety and its fickle freckles (who knows how?).

Glory be to God for dappled things –

The couple-color of the kingfisher's wings, adazzle and dim.

Glory be to God for dappled things –

And me. After all these years, believe it or not I am still surprised when I pass a full-length mirror and see my own little three-fingered hand, my short little arm in the mirror's honest reflection. A birth defect, they called it then. A fluke of birth that leaves me with eight instead of ten. I am in no way unhappy with my dappling – I've grown so accustomed to it there's no going back now – I'm just still in wonder over my unique making, even after all these years.

He fathers-forth whose beauty is without change: Praise Him.

If this is true, that He fathers us forth in beauty without change, then why do we fill our days with striving against the wonder?

We tuck and nip and tug and snip when the ironic beauty is found in the dappling.

John Donne (1572-1631)

Batter My Heart, Three-Person'd God

Batter my heart, three-person'd God, for you
As yet but knock, breathe, shine, and seek to mend;
That I may rise and stand, o'erthrow me, and bend
Your force to break, blow, burn, and make me new.
I, like an usurp'd town to another due,
Labor to admit you, but oh, to no end;
Reason, your viceroy in me, me should defend,
But is captiv'd, and proves weak or untrue.
Yet dearly I love you, and would be lov'd fain,
But am betroth'd unto your enemy;
Divorce me, untie or break that knot again,
Take me to you, imprison me, for I,
Except you enthrall me, never shall be free,
Nor ever chaste, except you ravish me.

Almost Repentant

At its best, spring is a season of introspection and tidying up. At least St. Augustine is honest about it, honest enough to not make excuses. He famously confesses, Lord, grant me chastity and continence, but not yet. His old loves, his hidden idols hold him back, tugging and whispering, Are you really getting rid of us? Don't you love us anymore? Please wait just a bit longer. Augustine realizes perhaps, at this time in his life, that he loves the search for truth more than the finding, more than the submission to it. I understand this; don't you?

In Shakespeare's *Hamlet,* King Claudius murders his brother and steals his brother's wife and crown. In Claudius' most important moment in the play, he confesses what he's done but in an empty room, only to himself. He is almost repentant, he almost gets there, crying out the honest question we all ask, what we desire perhaps more than anything else: may one be pardoned and retain the offense?

Realizing that the answer is, of course, *no*, Claudius tries another way. Bow, stubborn knees! he shouts with great noise and aplomb, hands raised. But alas, he remains standing. Unwilling to repent and save himself, he wanders away down the kingly corridor in the sorry consequences of his own sorry soul, sighing, *O wretched state! O bosom black as death! O limed soul that, struggling to be free, Art more engaged!*

He loved his sin more than he loved freedom, and in so doing he chose his own enslavement.

The fact that we've been given the gift of free will makes us more than puppets at the hand of a puppeteer. Exercising our freedom brings the consequences of our own making, both good and ill. We say we want the systems of our world to change, but perhaps we actually enjoy blaming the system since blame turns the responsibility outward. But nothing save the courage and unselfishness of individuals is going to make any system, large or small, work properly.

If people really acted on this in their daily lives, even just a few of us, a great deal would be changed.

ALMOST HOME

My little family is waiting – mother, brother, and me. The night my father is admitted to the ER in great pain, and we are not allowed to come in due to COVID-19 restrictions. Like a little train, our caravan of three cars follows the slow ambulance from the nursing facility and chug-chugs our uneventful way down Germantown Road to the Methodist Hospital in hopes of catching a glimpse of Geezer or even a hug before they whisk him inside and out of the cold. The nurse promised my mother she'd call when Geezer got a room. She promised us an update as soon as possible and gave my mother her cell phone number.

So, my little family, our little foursome *sans* one, stands outside of the ER in the parking lot, blanketed in the January mist to wait. No waiting room in these pandemic days, so what else can we do?

My brother fetches sandwiches for our impromptu parking lot picnic. My brother is good like that, he remembers my mother and I like pimento cheese. Even then, I think we all knew Geezer would not leave the hospital, although it's impossible to say these things out loud, especially in the beginning. My brother and I flank our mother – we all take the bread and eat it.

My father lived eleven more days.

The poets often voice our deepest thoughts, feelings we find hard to express. In his poem *Musée des Beaux Arts*, Auden pens,

> *How, when the aged are reverently, passionately waiting*
> *For the miraculous birth, there always must be*
> *Children who did not specially want it to happen…*

We are the children this time, standing in this cold, wet parking lot. We do not want this to happen.

Auden ponders not only the aged – who may be ready for the next inevitable steps – but also the children of the aged, the children of the dying, those folks standing outside in the January cold in a wet hospital parking lot eating pimento cheese sandwiches and watching over their mother and wondering what's happening inside the doors of the forbidden ER, not wanting any of this to happen.

But if Spring reminds us of anything, it is that we are not without hope, and we are not alone. The Resurrection narratives record how a totally new way of being has arisen in the universe. Something new.

Resurrection happened; resurrection happens.

I will not mock God with understatement. My father died. He slept and when he woke, he was Home. He walked through the door. My little family still stands together on the cold sod of earth, content for now to wait our turn.

SOMETHING NEW

I told the park ranger I wanted to see something new. I needed something new.

My family came to the Smoky Mountains most of the summers of my childhood. We were campers in those days, picknickers of the sort that always found a table close to the river; we liked the feel of the water's cool mist on our faces. When we were kids, my mother packed enormous lunches and we ate outside in the mountain air. People still talk about my mother's near-perfect chicken salad. I dare you to find better.

My brother and I spent long hours playing on the huge rocks in the Little Pigeon River, jumping from boulder to boulder, skipping stones. With our father, we tubed down the cold river from the jumping off spot to the fork in the river leading into Townsend. We hiked up to Clingman's Dome for the view of the blue mountains, then we pulled off to the side of the road to see it all again.

We could never get enough.

After my father's death in January, I felt a compulsion to get back to the mountains and see it all again, to drive along the winding roads and put my feet once again into the noisy river.

It's been too many years since I've come. But this time around, I felt the need to see something new, fresh and not yet seen, my soul needed a bit of resurrection. The park ranger suggested Abrams Falls, not the tallest waterfall in the park, but the one with the greatest volume of water. It's my favorite, the ranger grinned. The trail notes said that the path to the falls was "moderately difficult."

At the top of the mountain, the waterfall is as noisy as it is beautiful, splashing and whirling and singing in the busy joys of its falling, tumbling life. It's early spring now, and the mountain laurel on the path is not yet blooming – but the blooms will come again in these mountains. I've watched it all my life. The sparrow's eggs are not yet hatched, perhaps not yet laid – but new birds will sing again, for this is the way of things. The barren trees are still brown, not yet begun their greening – but their tender virgin leaves will open soon and spring into the warming light, for the time has come for the trees and flowers and birds and the creatures under the cold earth to wake, to come alive again.

These are the days of resurrection – the very earth in springtime proclaims this message that can be neither ignored nor denied nor disregarded. Only unseen. The natural processes of fall and winter and spring and summer can indeed be laborious, the paths through the seasons sometimes more than "moderately difficult" with all this living and dying and living again. But the truth of Spring is that one must die in order to live, and in that paradox dwells the hope the forest understands – nature is undaunted by this news.

Every day, Nature shouts the message of resurrection. This day I hear it in the waterfall's sweet, eternal song.

Does Not Wisdom Call?

Mrs. Lacy invites me to lunch on the first day of my substitute gig at St. Mary's. I am to teach tenth grade literature while Leigh is on maternity leave. Shall we meet in my classroom? the first of her many emails reads. Chair of the English department, I find Mrs. Lacy quite intimidating with her big black English-teacher glasses, her soft-spoken yet direct questions, and the sheer reputation of the school at large, especially the reputation of the English department which rests on her gentle shoulders; so I respond affirmatively and immediately. Of course, I type back. I can't wait.

Does not wisdom call? the Proverb asks. Indeed, it does, so we must train our ear to listen and to hear. Wisdom called to *me* on that day and asked me to lunch; she took her stand beside the gates and portals of St. Mary's School and cried aloud, offering me her instruction and knowledge. How could I not accept?

Stricken with Parkinson's a few years earlier, Mrs. Lacy's hand shakes only slightly as she holds her tome, teaching and leading her students into realms of gold and the beauty and wisdom of those who have gone before us – Shakespeare, Milton, Dostoevsky, a couple of Bronte sisters, and a grand slew of their companions – making a bit of sense of the present by examining what was written in the past. Is this not what great teachers do?

For what exactly is Hamlet asking anyway in his existential ponderings, *To die, to sleep – To sleep – perchance to dream. Ay, there's the rub!* We must dare to consider what dreams may come when we shuffle off this mortal coil; this ought to give us pause. And what of human freedom, Mr. Milton? *For so I created them free and free they must remain*, you declare in your epic of a paradise now lost. We must talk about human freedom, we must.

But by far the most powerful thought that I took with me when the substitute gig was finished belonged to Fyodor Dostoevsky – how could it be that I'd never read Dostoevsky before meeting Mrs. Lacy? Wisdom called out to me again in *The Brothers Karamazov*, where brother fights brother and father is killed and faith is wounded and nearly destroyed and the Christian existentialist Dostoevsky tells us that *God and the devil are fighting and the battlefield is the heart of man.* Oh wisdom, help us and protect us, guard our hearts for battle rages constant there.

"Keep the students in health of mind and soul and body," we pray each day in our school prayer. Amen.

And somehow, fifteen years pass. Mrs. Lacy retires and I now teach the seniors at St. Mary's and chair the department. I am forever glad that we have stayed in touch through these years.

Sometimes we meet for breakfast with our husbands – our two Larrys – just to talk; she, still teaching me, me, still learning from her. Does not understanding raise her voice? the Proverb asks. Parkinson's has placed my dear mentor in a wheelchair now, constant with movement. Her Larry pushes her gently to the table and they speak quiet words to each other almost continuously.

If you are not listening, you will miss it. One must listen when wisdom calls, for wisdom never shouts. We eat eggs and talk about literature. She has brought me a present, a copy of a definitive new book about the life and writings of Dostoevsky. I have come empty-handed – this seems to be our pattern. I come empty and she fills me.

Today we find ourselves talking again about the poetry of Gerard Manley Hopkins, our favorite poet. His odd diction and soft rhyme and gentle sprung rhythm. I would love to teach Hopkins to a group of students again, she says so quiet that I can barely hear her.

Do you feel up to it? Teaching all day is an exhausting practice, I remind her. Her Larry, a former philosophy professor, echoes the sentiment. I do. I really think I can do it, she says.

We make a plan.

A few weeks later, her Larry wheels Mrs. Lacy into my classroom on the third floor to teach Hopkins. The day is bright with April light and I am thankful I have a sunny room. I have prepped the students, my girls, for this day. I tell them of my friendship with Mrs. Lacy, her legacy at St. Mary's, and what these long years of friendship have come to mean to me. I tell them about her Parkinson's and what Parkinson's looks like so they won't be surprised. I tell them that I do not know how she might fare after a full day of teaching. I tell them about her love of beautiful language – like Lord Hamlet, she taught me how to love his words, words, words – and her love for me and how she revives in me a sense of wonder and always tickles my intellectual curiosity. And I tell them about my love for her. And my overwhelming gratitude. Unexpected tears flow and my students seem to understand. Their compassion flickers and they anticipate something they cannot name. Let's give Mrs. Lacy a day to remember, they all say.

The warm day arrives. Mrs. Lacy sits among my senior students up on the third floor. No wheelchair today. Today she chooses to sit in a student desk and opens her old tome and speaks her quiet words. I have discovered that profundity is almost always quiet. As I've said, wisdom rarely appears in the shouting or in the fray; hers is a soft voice.

My heart in hiding / Stirred for a bird

Mrs. Lacy – mother of five, master teacher, Parkinson's patient – and Gerard Manley Hopkins – Jesuit priest, philosopher, poetic innovator – join together to speak of the mysteries of life and teach young women one more time in a sunny classroom on the third floor. *My heart in hiding / Stirred for a bird,* Lacy and Hopkins say. The mystery of a heart stirring; have my students yet felt the stirring of a heart in hiding?

> *Now no matter, child, the name:*
> *Sorrow's springs are the same.*
> *Nor mouth had, no nor mind, expressed*
> *What heart heard of, ghost guessed:*
> *It is the blight man was born for,*
> *It is Margaret you mourn for.*

…these two say.

The mystery of mourning and sorrow and the fallenness of man. Have these young women yet felt this sting, and to what degree?

These two declare the mystery of the blindingly electric greatness of God. Who among my girls has been quiet enough yet to feel the charge of God's grandeur? Is it you? You?

Glory be to God for dappled things, say Hopkins and Lacy, awed at the mystery and terrible beauty of brokenness. Have any of the young minds in my classroom yet experienced or even pondered the precious gift of brokenness and the glory found in the dappled?

A woman broken by age and disease sits before them, riddled with constant movement, and she tells them that God is glorified in the variegated and the shattered. Book in hand, she and Hopkins form a chorus that sings of faith in something higher and stronger than circumstance, and certainly more beautiful. The students are moved by the moment and they ask Mrs. Lacy their questions. *Not* the questions they prepared for homework. No, no, not this day. The students ask real questions about life and hardship and age and blight and motherhood and sickness and springs of sorrow. My heart in hiding stirred.

By the end of the last class, we are all exhausted. Mrs. Lacy's Larry has stayed all day, tending to her, watching her, bringing her water, and helping her to reposition in the student desk. At times he would gently add a connecting word or two to the lesson. I watched his professorial face much of the day, a face of filled intense love, almost painfully so, for both the woman and the words. Perhaps the lesson between the man and the love of his life is the most profound of the day. Gerard Manley Hopkins would not have minded.

The last bell rings and the day is done. There are tears and reverie and understanding. Mrs. Lacy has spent some time each class period thanking the girls for their rapt attention and pertinent questions and for the chance to teach Hopkins again, an opportunity she thought long past. One of my morning students appears at my door in the late afternoon with a Thank-You note in tow. Unprompted, the girls had passed the hand-drawn card around all day during their break, all had signed. Sigh. People still do kind things and write words of thanks. Could these be the most important words of all? Is gratitude the greatest gift?

The girls have written their grateful words for Mrs. Lacy to take home with her. Thank you, Mrs. Lacy, for sharing your wisdom with us. Thank you for preparing this lesson for us. I didn't understand Hopkins at all until you came. I take the note and add just a few more words belonging to our favorite poet. Because my words pale, I lean on Hopkins for his.

The world is charged with the grandeur of God. It will flame out, like shining from shook foil …

Mrs. Lacy, Thank you for shining forth the grandeur of God, today and every day. Glory be to God.

Proverbs 8:1-3 – *Doth not wisdom call? and understanding put forth her voice? She standeth in the top of high places, by the way in the places of the paths. She crieth at the gates, at the entry of the city, at the coming in the doors.*

Larry helps his lovely wife back into her wheelchair, and tired, they head for home.

Gerard Manley Hopkins (1844-1899)

The Windhover

To Christ our Lord

I caught this morning morning's minion, king-
dom of daylight's dauphin, dapple-dawn-drawn Falcon, in his riding
Of the rolling level underneath him steady air, and striding
High there, how he rung upon the rein of a wimpling wing
In his ecstasy! then off, off forth on swing,
As a skate's heel sweeps smooth on a bow-bend: the hurl and gliding
Rebuffed the big wind. My heart in hiding
Stirred for a bird, – the achieve of, the mastery of the thing!

Brute beauty and valour and act, oh, air, pride, plume, here
Buckle! AND the fire that breaks from thee then, a billion
Times told lovelier, more dangerous, O my chevalier!

No wonder of it: shéer plód makes plough down sillion
Shine, and blue-bleak embers, ah my dear,
Fall, gall themselves, and gash gold-vermilion

LENT

SARTORIAL CHOICES

After the cold snows and the wild winter winds, Lent and Spring arrive on the same warm breath, these ironic hand-holding sisters of abstinence and fertility.

Lent asks me to look inward, to abstain perhaps, in order to ponder and consider the gifts. To be quiet and slow and intentional and still. To listen better and quit talking so much. To turn off the frantic, repetitive noise of the twenty-four-hour news cycle – who ever thought that was a good idea? – and ponder the small instead, look within. To practice seeing, and being, to at least try.

Spring asks of me the polar opposite. Fertile Spring roars onto the scene in grand fecundity, blooms everywhere, fragrance everywhere, new leaves bursting open in that special bright spring-green reserved for the earliest moments of the season's arrival. She's showing off, this Spring, putting on all her clothes in one dressing.

And yet a person can still miss it if her eyes focus in the wrong places. Perhaps, on the best of days with my practiced Lenten eye, I can see the gift, recognize the abundance and embrace it as what it is – Grace, neither earned nor deserved. Yet Spring asks me to throw my eyes and arms open as wide as they will go and clothe myself in all of the bloom and blossom and aroma and hope and newness of life. And what am I anyway, if I am not here to wear all of it, to throw grace around my shoulders and dance with it in the middle of the street, this abundance born again, shaken down and running over. We all are allowed our peculiar and particular sartorial choices.

Is this not gratitude? If not, what is? Is this not wisdom, or at least good sense? For with the measure I give, that will be measured back to me.

Like at the family cabin, after my father's funeral, when my grandson found ten or so of my father's hats and put them all on his head at the same time. Hats hidden, forgotten in the corners and crannies of an old man's closet but in due season found again in joy and remembrance. So why not put them all on, wear them all, all at once!

Like Spring.

Humble Stuff

Great patches of clover line the paths where I walk. Humble stuff, clover. Not showy like the cherry blossoms that shine for a magnificent moment and then vanish with the first winds. No, clover's got staying power, but it is easy to miss. Even though it reproduces itself in enormous patches of green, passersby are too often spellbound by the flashy tulips and the proud buttercups, overlooking the fine greenery growing silent and wild along the path.

When my father lay dying, a parade of doctors came and went. So many, of all shapes and variations, I had to take notes to keep up with them all and wrote their names and interests and physical descriptions in my journal: the neurologist wears his thick, black beard quite well, the Parkinson's specialist looks as young as one of my high school students, the cardiologist plays tennis with one of my colleagues at school. In the last days of the parade, though, a new doctor arrived who changed the game.

Dr. K comes in for the first time just minutes after the hospice nurse removes the rest of Geezer's monitors and the last of his IV bags, the impotent IV pole now left to stand watch over the dying.

I'm your father's attending now, Dr. K says simply. Noticing the empty pole at Geezer's bedside, she says, I see hospice has been in. She moves to Geezer's side. She lifts the sheet and glances at his bluing feet, she bends over his still body and listens to his labored breath. Satisfied with her brief observations, she takes a single step back from the bed railing, folds her hands gently in front of her, and speaks directly to my father, who has been unconscious now for several days. Dr. K tells my father how glad she is to meet him, how privileged she feels to attend to him in these days, and that it is she who will make sure he has all he needs to be comfortable.

This doctor speaks *to* the dying, not about him, not over him, not around him. And in her presence, I am not afraid. For several silent minutes every morning, Dr. K stands watch over my father. No words – for what is left to say? – just stillness. Her lack of hurry settles the room, offering silence as an antidote to the noisy machinery of living that demands our attention. Dr. K's silence demands nothing. Her quiet honors my father's life and dignifies his passing. After three or four full minutes, Dr. K tilts her head toward Geezer, smiles an easy smile, then bows to him before she goes. I miss her before she's closed the door.

Humility, in its dignity, is quite difficult to define. But in part, humility is quiet, unadulterated by worthless, prideful words. In the presence of humility, one feels less alone and less afraid. Humility, like a tiny breath of Heaven. Like clover.

William Blake (1757-1827)

Holy Thursday

Is this a holy thing to see,
In a rich and fruitful land,
Babes reduced to misery,
Fed with cold and usurous hand?

Is that trembling cry a song?
Can it be a song of joy?
And so many children poor?
It is a land of poverty!

And their sun does never shine.
And their fields are bleak & bare.
And their ways are fill'd with thorns.
It is eternal winter there.

For where-e'er the sun does shine,
And where-e'er the rain does fall:
Babe can never hunger there,
Nor poverty the mind appall.

The Least of These

In the levels of flower kingdom, the lowly dandelion dwells at the bottom rung. A common yard weed, dandelions plague the fancy Bermuda grass with their commonness and rapid proliferation. They are everywhere. The species we find in Memphis is listed in the "Lower Classifications," so yes, one can always descend in status. There is plenty of room at the bottom – always has been.

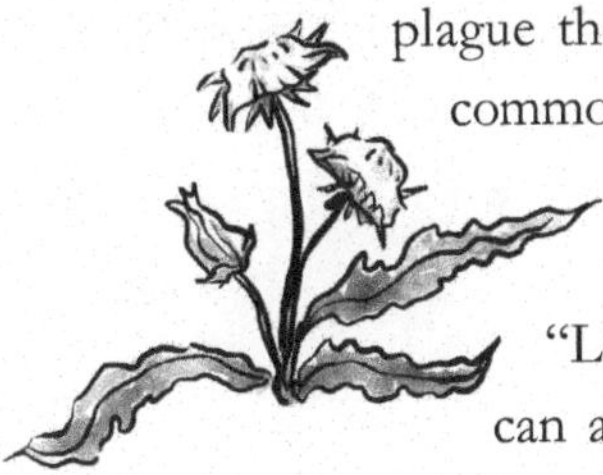

By Tuesday of the last week of Christ's life, the end of His earthly ministry was upon Him, and among His last words were instructions on the care of the least among us. Three times Jesus told the apostle Peter to go and feed them, and in so doing, he would be ministering to Christ.

Like, now, Peter. Go now.

What do we do about the poor among us in this highly evolved modern era of ours? We talk about poverty a great deal. We make some plans, take bills before legislation that will forever stall in forgotten cabinets because we've grown to love ourselves and our partisanship far more than we will ever love the poor.

We adore being on the right side – we love that stuff – worshipping at the altar of our own correctness just like the religious Temple leaders before us. Throwing stones at our enemies is a full-time job, so who-in-the-world has time for the poor?

Jesus told Peter to go and feed the poor. This is how He put it: feed someone. Give her something to drink. Invite her into your home. Clothe her. Care for her when she is sick. Visit her in prison.

And in doing these things for the least, we do them unto Him.

As always, there's a problem. We simply don't want to do this. We are lazy or judgmental or prejudiced or too busy or too tired. We prefer a quick miracle instead – where are those loaves and fishes when you need them?

Anyway, at the end of the day, isn't taking care of the poor God's job?

Where There is no Love, Put Love

In a large ceramic flower pot just outside my back porch, a little yellow plastic toy that somehow resembles both a lamb and a duck at the same time, has weathered the February snow storms in the space reserved for my geraniums. In a short month's time, this flower pot will be filled with bright red blooms, their tall spikey stalks raised heavenward in praise of warmer skies. But today, there is an unusual amount of snow for Memphis, and the little yellow toy is nearly covered in white.

There is a two-fold noteworthiness about this little plastic pot-dweller; one, we don't know where he came from or whose he is, and two, infinitely more important, we don't know what kind of animal he is. And this dilemma has become a source of much debate at the family dinner table. Is little guy a duck with a lamb's furry head and ears, or lamb with a duck's bill? Land-dweller or water-dweller, little one? Speak up. Mammal or fowl? Whose side are you on, anyway? It's hard to know sometimes. Either way, he's covered up to his neck in ice and snow, poor guy, and it's cold out there.

On the third snowy day, Teddy, my six-year-old grandson and love of my life, notices this stuck little creature and rescues him from his frozen plight. Together, Teddy and duck-lamb head indoors for a warm bath and a bite of lunch, and the boy and the snow creature sit together on the couch to watch a little Paw Patrol. Teddy's mother brings them warm tea.

As fortune would have it, the next day Teddy, the snow creature, and St Augustine of Hippo took a walk up the icy street. Hailing from warm North African regions, St. Augustine had not seen much snow in his lifetime and was quite interested in the slope of the sledding hill and the speeds Teddy had been able to attain, even on his first attempts at sledding. On the walk up the hill, the little snow-creature regaled Augustine with his lovely story of rescue from the cold and his new best friend Teddy, how Teddy took him in and gave him tea and how they sat together all afternoon on the orange couch, even though nobody knew what the snow creature was.

St Augustine nodded and smiled his simple reply – Where there is no love, put love, and you will draw out love. Teddy grinned.

But wait, you say. This story cannot yet be over. You never establish what the little creature actually is. You are the writer, you must identify him, classify him, pinpoint his differences, name our similarities so that we will know exactly what we are dealing with here. Is he a lamb with a duck's bill or a duck with a lamb's furry head and ears? The creature must choose. Speak up, we have to know!

I don't know. All I know is this. The humble and wise among us don't seem to require identification as a prerequisite to love.

Last Year's Geraniums

Last summer we grew the largest, healthiest geraniums we've ever grown. In large terra cotta pots right by the screen porch door, these beauties multiplied every day, it seemed, stretching their long skinny arms skyward, their red-petaled fingers opening anew every morning in the warmth of the bright morning sun.

Last weekend my husband planted this year's geraniums in the same pots by the same screen door.

At the moment these young plants are spindly and small, just a few humble blooms on short, stumpy stalks. Yet they stretch their thin arms upward nonetheless, in faith I suppose, and bow their heads to the inevitable rain, somehow knowing all these things work together for their good growth.

I'm pretty sure this year's geraniums have already heard the secret of the stunning success of last year's flowers. One quiet afternoon last summer I overheard their whispers on the warm spring breezes; these new young plants hear it on this year's breeze and don't seem worried about a thing, even today's unexpected cold spring rain.

Want to know the secret? I can tell you what I overheard. Last year's geraniums said the secret of good growth is to rejoice in the glory of all the flowers, not just the ones in the same species, for variety adds depth and wisdom to the garden. The beauty is in the variety, *not* the sameness. The old advised the new to set down pride in their own beauty so they can recognize the unique blooms and scents of their neighbors as excellent things, to not fear the differences in species, for only in such humility will they find contentment.

They said, and this is of utmost importance, to love the begonia and the petunia as you love yourself. Rid yourself of the vile weed of jealousy – they shouted this part – root jealousy out at all costs for this is an indulgence that brings only despair, and the garden is simply too glorious to spend all our days and ways in the despair of comparison.

If this year's geraniums learn to love their neighbors as themselves, then, and only then, will they grow to love themselves as their neighbors. In this lovely patch of the garden will they grow content.

I think my new geraniums heard the secret of good, happy growth. I hope they embrace the secret.

We shall see, for one knows a contented flower when she sees one, just as she recognizes discontent within the garden. It's not hard to spot.

Nineteen Minutes

Hey, Ba. Would you like to sit with me and watch the laundry? Sitting cross-legged in front of my front-loading washing machine, my grandson invites me to join him, to watch the laundry spin.

I sit beside him on the floor and he crawls into my lap, his curly head against my chest – he, characteristically interested in the workings of machines of all kinds, uncharacteristically quiet on this unexpected snowy day, home from school. On the floor of my laundry room, through the dim glass, he and I watch the clothes spin.

In one hand he holds the pinkish ribbon of the Valentine's balloon his great-grandmother Nanny bought for him on a whim at the grocery store. I know how T loves balloons, she'd said, still numb from the death of her beloved a short month prior. The pink balloon still held enough helium to tug slightly toward the heavens.

With his other hand he takes mine and places it on his face, my cue to trail my fingers through his hair and tickle his cheek with my fingertips. And for nineteen rare, quiet minutes, he and I watch the world spin.

Somewhere around minute sixteen, he starts to sing. I lean forward to hear. The whispered song is not for me but rather for the day, or for himself, or perhaps for these precious, unhindered minutes on a snowy day.

I see the last vestiges of his chubby babyhood disappearing on the back of his hand. This is the hand of a boy now, a boy who built a snowman yesterday with his daddy and made two baskets last week at basketball.

If Lent is about anything meaningful, perhaps part of the practice is about watching without judgment, active loving without boundary. Relinquishing pretense. To sit still, or stiller, before the spinning world and remember that we are not alone here.

The timer on the washer says one minute. I know when the buzzer sounds, the moment will end. All things end, bad and good. But for these nineteen minutes, we sit quict together, grandmother and grandson, his head in my lap, and it is a fine, good thing on a cold day.

THREE WOMEN BY THE NILE

Three women saved the baby's life that morning. Throw every newborn Hebrew boy into the Nile River! demands Pharaoh, yet another fearful despot in the very long line of oppressors that stretches from the beginning of Time until Time's last day. But one Hebrew mother says *no.* Moses' mother looks at her baby and sees that he is special, then she acts in faith. In desperation complete, this ingenious mother weaves a basket of reedy papyrus, places her infant in the bottom of the basket, and floats him right down the river.

Pharaoh's own daughter does the same. She notices the floating basket, sees the Hebrew boy, then acts in faith, drawing the special child from the river's clutch and claiming him for her own. And from the edge of the river, Moses' sister follows suit, witnessing the rescue from the bullrushes. Another courageous woman, a slave girl, asks the daughter of the despot himself, Shall I find a Hebrew mother to nurse the baby for you?

And God takes care of the salvation.

I have one question. Is it the way the baby looks that makes him special, his actual appearance, or rather the way his mother views him? In my book, this is an important question. Perhaps

Moses looks like an ordinary Hebrew baby, but because these women see him as special, they act in faith to save him. Perhaps everyone is to be saved in this way.

If Lent is meant to be a slower season, then perhaps it is meant to be a season of seeing. Perhaps the discipline, the very act of trying to view all the people of this world as special, as fearfully and wonderfully made like Moses's mother and Pharoah's daughter and Moses's sister saw him, then looking at creation and the people inhabiting this place as unique and beautiful and worthy is one of the truest acts of faith.

What if we set anger and judgment down for a season, as a Lenten practice, and take a look around through newer glasses, better lenses that magnify love instead of cynicism. Or at least try, before our time is done, before our light is spent.

Seeing precedes acting. Acting that precedes seeing is surely the definition of despotism.

Each Its Own and None the Same

Since my trek up Mt. LeConte in the early spring, I've been thinking about immeasurability.

The natural world is rife with itself. There's simply so much of it.

Along the mountain path, common mosses grow lush atop fallen trees and stumps, cushiony lichens clothe thin, long branches of the slender trees, and the cool stones are covered in velvety green cushions. All of this beauty enough to stop and sit and stare for more hours than I have, if I remember to bring my seeing eyes with me on the hike. There are over 12,000 known species of mosses in creation. The moss I photographed on the mountain is named sphagnales.

My nose to the dirt, I look closely at the moss; there are acres and acres of it, miles and miles! Every inch of the mountain forest carpeted with tiny green arms sending their skinny fingers upward, reaching reaching in praise of the warming spring sun, glistening in the morning light, each tiny waxy finger its own and none the same.

And the snowflakes along the last leg before the summer, the icy flakes of winter's final protest – so many, so many!

Infinite numbers piling up in inches and feet under the ever-dark canopy of the dense forest, each flake unique, fragile, and temporary. None the same; I cannot fathom.

Immeasurable! – so vast that if I think about it too much, I need to sit down.

And don't get me started again about the stars. Scientists estimate there are 100 billion stars in our Milky Way galaxy alone – although apparently, they argue about this estimation, some astronomers declaring at least four times that many. And there are 200 billion to two trillion galaxies in the observable universe. Immeasurable! – so vast that if I think about it too much, I need to sit down. A mere glance at a photograph taken from the Hubble or James Webb telescopes and my knees buckle. Each one its own and not one the same.

The Population Reference Bureau (PRB) estimates that 108 billion people have been born on planet Earth, and by 2050, the number will be 113 billion. Who can know?

I know only one thing, that I am here. We are here midst this profound immeasurability, each one of us and not one created the same – and somehow that matters. Thornton Wilder's play *Our Town* asks the question, *Do human beings ever realize life while they live it? – every, every minute?* The answer, of course, is no. *Saints and poets maybe . . . they do some.*

Well, I am neither saint nor poet, but I find when I consider my place amidst the vast vastness and singularity and precision and sheer raw numbers involved in the study of and observation of and awe of creation, all I've got left is humility, and I suppose that's a fine enough place to start.

Samuel Taylor Coleridge (1772-1834)

Work Without Hope

All Nature seems at work. Slugs leave their lair -
The bees are stirring - birds are on the wing -
And Winter slumbering in the open air,
Wears on his smiling face a dream of Spring!
And I the while, the sole unbusy thing,
Nor honey make, nor pair, nor build, nor sing.

Yet well I ken the banks where amaranths blow,
Have traced the fount whence streams of nectar flow.
Bloom, O ye amaranths! bloom for whom ye may,
For me ye bloom not! Glide, rich streams, away!
With lips unbrightened, wreathless brow, I stroll:
And would you learn the spells that drowse my soul?

Work without Hope draws nectar in a sieve,
And Hope without an object cannot live.

PUSHING

Springtime reminds us that life is, in part, about pushing. The pink tulip must push her way out of her tight green-bud before coming into the cool blue morning air. The caterpillar must wriggle and shove her way out of her thick, crusty cocoon as she transforms into something entirely new. The tiny white crocus must butt her way up through the damp brown mud in order to feel the sun's warm glow.

And Sisyphus, our mythical Everyman, rolls his boulder up the mountain every single morning only to have it to roll back down again at the end of the day. Every day the same – pushing, pushing, pushing. And yet, the myth imagines Sisyphus happy.

How can this be? I shout into the abyss. How in the world can Sisyphus be happy? Is it really as simple as choosing happiness in the sheer mundanity of everyday life? Choosing joy midst all this struggle, all this pushing? Am I so lazy – or is this pride? – that I think I deserve joy simply because I am here, that I don't have to push for joy like everything else? Must I really work for joy, must I choose it every minute?

The natural world – the tulip and the butterfly and the crocus – seems to say *yes* to this question. The push toward joy is worth the work, they sing. Old Sisyphus nods his assent with a grin as he turns and heads back down his ironic mountain to do it all again in the morning.

John Donne (1572-1631)

Death, Be Not Proud

Death, be not proud, though some have called thee
Mighty and dreadful, for thou art not so;
For those whom thou think'st thou dost overthrow
Die not, poor Death, nor yet canst thou kill me.
From rest and sleep, which but thy pictures be,
Much pleasure; then from thee much more must flow,
And soonest our best men with thee do go,
Rest of their bones, and soul's delivery.
Thou art slave to fate, chance, kings, and desperate men,
And dost with poison, war, and sickness dwell,
And poppy or charms can make us sleep as well
And better than thy stroke; why swell'st thou then?
One short sleep past, we wake eternally
And death shall be no more; Death, thou shalt die.

The Ups and Downs of Leaving

Yesterday I sat in a chapel service in St. Mary's Cathedral in Memphis, listening to the president of the senior class of the school where I teach give a lovely talk to her classmates about *leaving*, how the inevitable process of leaving was upon the group of soon-to-be high school graduates. And the tears began to flow.

A good friend of mine, whose father went into hospice at about the same time, sent me a text that read, Dad is beginning the ups and downs of leaving. What apt and accurate phrasing my friend employed, how clearly she understands the processes of leaving this earth, the fact that this is not our home, neither is this the end.

We live in a world where leaving is the end game. Every year all my wonderful students leave. We rear our children to grow up and leave. We leave one job for another, one city for another, one person for another. Everyone eventually leaves this place, no one stays put, no one stays here. And the tears and anguish and grief in all these passings are, at the end of the day, tears of inevitability. For despite our constant protestations, everyone leaves.

On Good Friday, Jesus left. But the Christian story offers the promise of another system, a place, after this one, where leaving dies, and all that is left is life. Death, thou shalt die, the poet said. I guess that's why we call this Friday *good*.

Alfred, Lord Tennyson (1809-1892)

The Lady of Shalott Part II

There she weaves by night and day
A magic web with colours gay.
She has heard a whisper say,
A curse is on her if she stay
To look down to Camelot.
She knows not what the curse may be,
And so she weaveth steadily,
And little other care hath she,
The Lady of Shalott.

And moving thro' a mirror clear
That hangs before her all the year,
Shadows of the world appear.
There she sees the highway near
Winding down to Camelot:
There the river eddy whirls,
And there the surly village-churls,
And the red cloaks of market girls,
Pass onward from Shalott.

But in her web she still delights
To weave the mirror's magic sights,
For often thro' the silent nights
A funeral, with plumes and lights
And music, went to Camelot:
Or when the moon was overhead,
Came two young lovers lately wed:
"I am half sick of shadows," said
The Lady of Shalott.

Sick of Shadows

Stories of isolation are not new. Remember Rapunzel? Trapped in tall tower so long her hair grew to the ground below. And Snow White, hiding in a cottage from a jealous, wicked queen.

And lonely Leah, Jacob's first wife, the unpreferred, not as beautiful as her sister.

And you and me, to varying degrees, quarantined in our months and months of the modern plague.

Alfred, Lord Tennyson writes about a woman in isolation, the Lady of Shalott, cursed, sitting alone at her loom in a lofty tower above Camelot, watching life from a high, distant window.

And moving thro' a mirror clear
That hangs before her all the year,
Shadows of the world appear.

Shadows of the world. We were not created to live in the shadows. The Lady of Shalott had some gumption, though. She paid attention to the world outside her window, and yearned to join – or rejoin – the damsels clad and the curly shepherd-lad. She listened to the river's living song.

I'm half sick of shadows, she finally said.

I'm half sick of shadows, she finally said. We were neither created nor intended to dwell in our shadows. Shadows of unforgiveness. Shadows of fear. Shadows of hatred. Shadows of bitterness. Shadows of despair. Shadows of a former, better self.

The Lady of Shalott dared to free herself from her life in the shadows. She dared leave the cursed tower behind.

> *She left the web, she left the loom,*
> *She made three paces thro' the room,*
> *She saw the water-lily bloom…*

She chose to LIVE, until she died.

So. What about me, and you? Do we want to really live before we die? Then we must practice the opposite of death. We must live, forgive, grieve, love, believe, get up, get out, embrace, pray, try, pursue joy, lay down hate, lay down bias, lay down demands, lay down the sins we love. Practice resurrection and live, live, live, live, live until we die.

We are children of the Almighty God, the God of light and fire. We were not created to remain in these shadows. This is the message of grace.

Gerard Manley Hopkins (1844-1899)

Spring

Nothing is so beautiful as Spring –
  When weeds, in wheels, shoot long and lovely and lush;
  Thrush's eggs look little low heavens, and thrush
Through the echoing timber does so rinse and wring
The ear, it strikes like lightnings to hear him sing;
  The glassy pear tree leaves and blooms, they brush
  The descending blue; that blue is all in a rush
With richness; the racing lambs too have fair their fling.

What is all this juice and all this joy?
  A strain of the earth's sweet being in the beginning
In Eden garden. – Have, get, before it cloy,
  Before it cloud, Christ, lord, and sour with sinning,
Innocent mind and Mayday in girl and boy,
  Most, O maid's child, thy choice and worthy the winning.

Nothing Is So Beautiful As Spring

In the first stanza of Hopkins' poem entitled "Spring," the poet exalts the beauty and grandeur of Springtime, *when weeds, in wheels, shoot long and lovely and lush* and *the blue is all in a rush / With richness.*

I've been photographing these weeds and wheels all season thus far, and of course the poet is correct in his assertion that *nothing is so beautiful as spring.*

But it's the question in the second stanza that plops me flabbergasted into my chair. *What is all this juice and all this joy?* the poet asks, the question all thinkers ask, all philosophers ponder, about which all writers write.

What is this? What is going on here?

Is there meaning in all this beauty, all the juice and all this joy?

What are we doing here?

Our first home was a garden, Hopkins reminds us, *Earth's sweet being in the beginning.*

But we have stained the garden with our fantastic human arrogance, haven't we? Are we still denying this? Who can deny we have trod down the soil, smudged Creation with our constant strain of having and getting before our enemy claims it first, clouding our skies and souring our hearts, *Have, get, before it cloy / Before it cloud.*

Like spoiled children who eat all the candy and make ourselves sick on the demands of our own slant will rather than share a bit, even just a bit of sweetness with our brothers.

What I love most about Gerard Manley Hopkins is his fearless reminder to return to the origin.

In his poetry exists the call to come on back home. Hopkins asks us to remember the *maid's child,* Mary's boy, who is *thy choice and worth the winning.*

On Thursday of Holy Week, Maundy Thursday, Christ eats His last meal.

Tomorrow He dies.

Once a thing gets rolling, it doesn't take long to crucify a person.

Perhaps I'll join the crowd at the foot of the cross, beneath those forest timbers felled to kill a Man of paradox who claimed light in the darkness and joy in pain and life in death. But if I do join the few women who gathered on that hard day, I will know what the pair of Marys did not – this is not the end of this story.

Nothing is so beautiful as spring.

To Be or Not To Be

Hamlet is famous for the line, *To be or not to be, that is the question.* But what exactly is the question?

The existential dilemma is, in part, the question of how to live, how to be, and whether or not my choices make a hill of beans of difference. Am I choosing well or ill? Good or evil?

Choice – Eden's gift, mankind's dilemma. Every time I make a choice, I sharpen the choice-making part of myself, I alter my own being into something a little different that it was before. Thus, all life long, just like the heroes and monsters in literature, I am slowly turning myself in one direction or another, turning myself into a more heavenly being or a more hellish one. I am becoming, by my own volition, more in harmony with God and others or more in a state of war with God and others. I am choosing to be a creature of joy and peace and power or to be a creature of rage and madness and impotence.

This is the human situation; this is my choice.

The poet T.S. Eliot explains the condition as having the choice to live a life centered on hate or centered on love. So, it turns out I get to choose what will consume my life, what I will become. Consumed by the fire of love and its passions or the fire of hate and its passions.

The only choice left is apathy, which is not being at all.

Gerard Manley Hopkins (1844-1899)

As Kingfishers Catch Fire

As kingfishers catch fire, dragonflies draw flame;
As tumbled over rim in roundy wells
Stones ring; like each tucked string tells, each hung bell's
Bow swung finds tongue to fling out broad its name;
Each mortal thing does one thing and the same:
Deals out that being indoors each one dwells;
Selves – goes itself; myself it speaks and spells,
Crying Whát I dó is me: for that I came.

I say móre: the just man justices;
Keeps grace: thát keeps all his goings graces;
Acts in God's eye what in God's eye he is –
Chríst – for Christ plays in ten thousand places,
Lovely in limbs, and lovely in eyes not his
To the Father through the features of men's faces.

A Thought On Lesser Gods (1)

In his poem "Kingfishers Catch Fire," poet Gerard Manley Hopkins writes this stanza:

> *Each mortal thing does one thing and the same:*
> *Deals out that being indoors each one dwells;*
> *Selves – goes itself; myself it speaks and spells,*
> *Crying What I do is me: for that I came.*

Not an easy stanza, granted, but message awaits the patient pilgrim.

Hopkins reminds us that what is inside of us, the part of us (we think) we keep *indoors* will always always always find its way out of doors by what we do. Our actions bespeak us (didn't our mothers tell us this from our youngest days?) – *Myself it speaks and spells.*

What I do is me, the poet declares in bold clear straightforward words – not what I say or what I claim to do or what I convince myself I do or what I wish I did or what I should do or what I tell those around me I do. But what I actually *do.*

Part of the great deception is that we think we can hide our innards. We live and breathe under the false impression that we dwell among the extraordinary, those who can camouflage their insides with the outside trappings of fashion and fancy, and then we justify these myths-of-our-own-making. But the truth remains nonetheless – no matter our attempts to dress and redress, what is hidden in the dark inside blooms bright in the light of day.

The hot sun uncovers and the unblind world sees – what I *do* is me, for this I came.

Consider the lily with her large, flared white-trumpet. I step into my garden and she shouts who she is by what she *does* – she blooms. For this she came.

Consider the bee. What he does is him, dancing all the livelong day from bloom to bloom, gathering his nectar for the good of hive and queen, doing his work. For this he came.

Consider the ant who has neither commander nor overseer nor ruler nor king, yet stores his provisions in summer and gathers his food at harvest. For this he came.

What is on the inside blooms out, dances out, works out. We only are what we are on the inside.

We humans, in love with our rational logical thought, tend to believe we are above the laws of nature, that we are *extra*-ordinary; the ancient cup of literature overflows with doomed characters who think themselves above the natural law of reaping and sowing. And we, we odd characters who live at this very moment in time, we saturate our minds with fearful musings then weep and complain because we find no joy.

We fill our minds with the lesser acrimonious gods of criticism and anger and demands and resentment, then we wonder why we feel so alone.

We fill our minds with hate then cancel God for the lack of love in the world.

O, humankind, how irrational is our reason! O bud, O ant, O bee, how much wiser you are than we!

Perhaps the most tempting of all the lesser gods is rationalization. We worship daily at the broken altar of excuse-making and chant in adoration this unholy catechism: I am unique and thus above logical, natural consequences of existence.

What a myth, a Siren's song if there ever was one, and we've been falling for it since the beginning. For this we came? No, dear God, no. There's more, there's more.

Thank God for resurrection, Easter's promise.

Thank God for restoration; for this, Christ came.

Oscar Wilde (1854-1900)

E Tenebris

Come down, O Christ, and help me! Reach thy hand,
For I am drowning in a stormier sea
Than Simon on thy lake of Galilee:
The wine of life is spilt upon the sand,
My heart is as some famine-murdered land,
Whence all good things have perished utterly,
And well I know my soul in Hell must lie
If I this night before God's throne should stand.
"He sleeps perchance, or rideth to the chase,
Like Baal, when his prophets howled that name
From morn to noon on Carmel's smitten height."
Nay, peace, I shall behold before the night,
The feet of brass, the robe more white than flame,
The wounded hands, the weary human face.

A Thought On Lesser Gods (2)

Before Holy Week begins, I need to determine who it is I worship, or what.

The children of Israel found fault with Moses and his God, those two simply didn't move quickly enough to suit the anxious desert crowd. The people's patience ran thin with Moses when he stayed too long on the mountain receiving the commandments from God – forty whole days! How long does it take to receive the very words of God, for heaven's sake! Why is Moses so slow? – so the angry crowd snatched their jewelry from their wrists and necks and ankles and flung all that gold into a furious fire and demanded another god, one that tended to their immediate desires.

There are plenty enough of those, to be sure.

Moses' brother Aaron, out of his enormous fear of man, fashioned a god that met the people's demands, a god of logic and human design, a golden cow in the likeness of the Egyptian bull-god Apis – a familiar god, one the people could see, fashioned out of the conditional demands of impatient people. And the people danced around the thing and touched it and bowed before it and worshipped it, as all people are so quick and wont to do.

This story begs the question, is God not supposed to be a higher power? Is a god not to be something (or Someone) bigger than us and our faulty human logic and weak, demanding, sluggish natures?

Lesser gods interest me in their promises of comfort, in their promises of taking the pressure off when the God of Heaven seems silent and far removed. But a nagging question lies at the core of the argument: from what source do lesser gods spring?

Perhaps lesser gods spring from the needy coils of the human heart – impatience and pride and jealousy and covetousness and envy and the demands of ego and self-satisfaction and, above all, immediacy.

Of our gods, we demand comfort immediate, at the very least.

Faith in the God of Easter is not a warm blanket, for this God is neither immediate nor predictable nor simple; if these are our demands, we have no choice but to sate our exigencies with plentiful lesser gods.

Faith in the God of Easter is the cross, which is neither simple nor predictable nor immediate; nay, just the opposite. So, before Holy Week begins, I need to determine who or what it is I love and worship before I go about singing songs of praise and waving palm branches to a God I really don't know or worship or trust.

Gerard Manley Hopkins (1844-1899)

Giver of Life

From "The Wreck of the Deutschland"

Thou mastering me
God! giver of breath and bread;
World's strand, sway of the sea;
Lord of living and dead;
Thou hast bound bones & veins in me, fastened me flesh,
And after it almost unmade, what with dread,
Thy doing: and dost thou touch me afresh?
Over again I feel thy finger and find thee.

A THOUGHT ON LESSER GODS (3)

Before Holy Week begins, it might be a good practice for me to name a few of my own personal lesser gods lest I miss the entire point of the holiest week in the Christian calendar and render the practice vain, or worse, a mockery. Perhaps I should acknowledge the existence of at least a few of these little gods, for can one shed a thing she denies?

What about the lesser god of my impatience which I indulge so freely when my lunch arrives late or cold or if my proper seat at the lunch table is in any way disturbed or when I am in any way inconvenienced or when the salad bar at school doesn't have tuna salad and everyone knows I eat tuna salad every day for lunch, how hard is it to make a little tuna salad!

Or the little god of my quick anger to which I attend with great care and choose to deem as righteous and even holy with my glib phrases of how Jesus himself was angry at the cleansing of His temple – what daring gall have I to make such comparisons! – oh, and also the lesser god of my own gall.

Or the sacrifices I make daily on the altar of my own self-importance, the worship of the essential need of me in the good work of the world, the gilded armor of my own demands, my rights, armor I don on the daily to protect myself against this harsh, competitive world.

Or the competitive nature of my own pride, for buying into the deception that meaning and influence is not found in being rich or clever or pretty or smart but rather in being richer and cleverer and prettier and smarter. Lord, help me.

As long as I continue to elevate myself above others, which is the true god and temptation of this world, then at least I must acknowledge that the only way I can view things and people is down. And of course, as long as I am looking down, I cannot see anything above me.

Lent is the reminder that Someone is indeed greater than I and worthy of my setting aside the lesser things.

Glory

On Mount Sinai, the mountain where the Lord dwelled, Moses stood before the glory of God and besought God for his miracle, the desire of his human heart – Show me your glorious presence.

God answered Moses' earnest request that day, saying, I will make my goodness pass before you, and I will announce my name, the LORD, so you can hear it. God's glorious presence passed by Moses, hiding in the crevice of the rocks, as men are apt to do when God arrives. God covered Moses' face with His hand and allowed the mere man to see a glimpse of the backside of His glory, for to view God's face would be sure death.

Moses *saw* God.

I read this passage again and again during Lent and realize that I, like Moses, know what I want.

I want to see God's glory. I want to stand before a bush ablaze. I want to meet Him on His mountain and hear him say His own name. I want to see these miracles, and right this minute would be fine timing as far as I'm concerned.

And yet the handiwork of God sprawls ever before me, His finger everywhere I look. Not only in the raw beauty of the orange blossom and the pink bud and the blue-blue sky, but in the mechanism of creation acting in accordance to its created nature. My friend photographed a praying mantis standing in glorious splendor, proud atop his leaf, moving in the fullness of his unique creation.

In the photograph one sees the shimmery camouflage of the mantis' leafy green color, the thinner green-brown of his bulbous eyes, his strong and busy arms bent in prayer, the complex symmetry of his spindly legs. And he, just one of the innumerable simple, ordinary created things, yet nothing about the smallest created thing is simple, nothing ordinary. It's all miracle. If I am not careful, I could worship the creature rather than his Creator, for to witness His glory overwhelms.

Wherever we turn our eyes, Creation shines. God's goodness passes ever before us. Who among us has the courage to see it?

So, what tiny sacrifice might I offer this Lent to the One who reveals His glory to me every day? I'll try to open my eyes, I'll try to see His glory with gratitude. Perhaps I'll even raise up my hands and muster up a bit of praise. At the very least I'll remove my shoes, for this is indeed holy ground.

Christina Rossetti (1830-1894)

Easter Even

The tempest over and gone, the calm begun,
Lo, "it is finished," and the Strong Man sleeps:
All stars keep vigil watching for the sun,
The moon her vigil keeps.

A garden full of silence and of dew,
Beside a virgin cave and entrance stone:
Surely a garden full of Angels too,
Wondering, on watch, alone.

They who cry "Holy, Holy, Holy," still
Veiling their faces round God's Throne above,
May well keep vigil on this heavenly hill
And cry their cry of love.

Adoring God in His new mystery
Of Love more deep than hell, more strong than death;
Until the day break and the shadows flee,
The Shaking and the Breath.

A Pair of Marys

What can I add to the Easter story that has not already been said in these past two millennia? Nothing really. Except it was brought to my attention in a new way recently how in the Jesus narratives, God uses two women to give birth to His story.

First God entrusts a young woman, a virgin named Mary to carry the very Gospel in her womb.

And then, on the day of resurrection, God entrusts another woman named Mary, from Magdala, to carry the miraculous news of the resurrection, the Gospel, to the disciples: *Go to my brothers and tell them*, the risen Christ said to Mary.

I don't know how long it took Mary Magdalene to run from the tomb back to the town where the disciples lived, I don't know this distance. But for that period of time, as the redeemed woman ran, she was the only person in the entire world who knew the truth, that the dead had risen. She alone carried the good news that changed the entire world – I stagger at this thought. The weight of the Gospel itself, the future of the Church, and the knowledge of the resurrected Christ lay in the hands of one single, human being – a broken, humble woman who simply believed the promise of life after death. She told her story, and the world changed.

Oh, what a unique and marvelous story is this Gospel. On Easter Sunday, many of us are thinking of our loved ones in Heaven; I join you in this bittersweet reminiscing. It's impossible to imagine what all those saints are doing up there in Heaven, your beloved and mine. But at the very least, they are alive, more alive than they ever were here.

Can you even imagine their dancing with abandon before the throne of God with Mary and Mary and Peter and John and Teresa of Avila and Mother Teresa and Augustine and Martin Luther and John the Baptist and your precious beloved one and my sweet father, their hands lifted in praise, all dancing and singing the truest truth, *I know that my Redeemer lives.*

Easter changes everything.

SUMMER

The Black Hole

I was the only woman aboard. The guys were all fist-pumping and chanting and glancing over the side of the dive boat, looking hard into the deep blue water for an early glimpse of the great reef where we were to dive that day. The dive master had promised us a spectacular sight and we were ready, and intrigued. Well, the men were intrigued, *pumped* and *stoked* I believe were the terms they favored. I, on the other hand, the only novice diver among us, had a few cautious questions before this dive began.

You say this dive is called The Black Hole, I began, talking over the dive master's shoulder as he sped the boat to the dive spot. Could you tell me just a little more about it? I've just completed my lessons and got my certification, but that was in the North Sea, in the Netherlands, where you don't go deep and there are no real reefs. Did I hear you say that the Black Hole spits a diver out at a bit more than 100 feet? Well, I've never been to that depth and maybe I should sit this first one out, just let the guys go, and I'll take the shallower dive later. Don't you think?

I asked many questions but soon realized there was only one answer, for the die had already been cast; I stepped onto this boat, and this boat was diving The Black Hole.

This lady doth protest too much.

The dive master's answers to me came in his lovely rich Caribbean brogue and were all the same, identical really, whether we were discussing seasickness or diving into deep holes in the reef or how long we would actually stay under the water or if there would be any snacks after the dive is done. Probably world politics and a world-wide pandemic would elicit the same response from him – Ah, all is good, mon, no worries. I'll be there with you.

We were a party of six. Larry and me, Larry's brother, two college guys from the University of Georgia, wearing T-shirts to prove it, and the dive master. The day was perfect for diving – not much wind and thus very few waves. The turquoise ocean seemed ready to receive us and, for this moment, it was easy. And beautiful.

Ah, we are here, mon, the dive master announced, turning off the skiff's motor and tying onto a bouncing buoy marker, the pre-dive stillness broken with the stirrings and whirrings of equipment prep, masks and flippers and tanks and belts and weights and one guy had a knife, now what's that about? Let it be noted that while we wore equipment Jacques Cousteau surely would have coveted and enough of it to stay underwater for the rest of our lives, the dive master donned only his tank and regulator, and a mask with no strap – he held the mask on his face by taking a hard, deep breath just before diving in. Oh yeah, and some pitiful-looking, half-splintered flippers. He was a real no-frills kind of guy.

Here's what we'll do, our dive master began his brief tutorial. You will flip off the back of this boat, one at a time. Wait for me just under the surface, ten or fifteen feet down. We'll go down to eighty feet where the mouth of the Black Hole is. You must watch the water change colors, for the blues get deeper and richer as you descend, so very beautiful. Keep your eyes wide open and don't miss the fishes and always look both up and down as you descend. When we get to about eighty feet, you will see the great hole in the reef. It is a very dark cave and you will see no light when you enter it, but that's OK, mon, just swim in, no worries. The path will quickly dogleg a bit to the right, and it is then you will see light. Swim toward that light. The end of this reef cave will spit you out over water thousands of feet deep, and the dark blue water of the depths combined with the light blue water above will create for you a color that you can see nowhere else on earth. It's like a blue from heaven, you must see it to know it's real. That's why we go to the Black Hole, to see that blue.

The two college boys finished gearing-up first and started a low, growling chant of Black Hole, Black Hole, like a football warm-up, I suspect, hitting their knees with their eager fists, and then in they jumped and the rest of us followed, rolling in backwards, adjusting masks and regulators. From now on, hand and eye communication only.

The slow descent to eighty feet was like a floating dream; sea turtles eased past us as they did in antiquity, unafraid of human touch, and schools of tiny, neon fishes darted by, flitting with color, fins large and small. Weightless wanderers were we, journeying to a new place for the first time, as the poet Keats observed in his line, *[like] a new planet swims into his ken.*

The journey to the reef was quicker than I expected, my new environs just glanced upon, no time for proper examination, and we all soon found ourselves hovering above the cave, peering into its small entrance, maybe ten feet in diameter, twelve tops. Floating, we divers glanced at our dive master, needy for his wordless instructions. Glancing downward into the Black Hole, he pointed with authority and nodded into the darkness. We had already received our instructions on the boat: the cave tunnel will quickly dogleg a bit to the right and then you will see the light. Swim toward that light.

Nodding and grinning, the dive master modeled his own teaching and, with great speed and agility, turned from us and swam into the pitch of the black hole – I blinked and he was gone. The college guys followed suit, as did my brother-in-law. Down down down they went, simply disappearing into the reef one after the other, the great mouth swallowing them all so profoundly that Larry and I were simply left behind, hovering above the black. I needed another moment to look around me, to be sure that they really were gone. They were. It happened so fast and the hole was much much blacker than I expected.

I cannot do this, my frightened eyes said to Larry, pleading for mercy and a way out. This is much more than I bargained for, it's way too dark in there – no light at all. We have to go, Larry's eyes replied in return, there is no other way, we are too far from the dive boat.

He is staying behind so that I won't be alone here. What else can he do? We must follow the others, his eyes said, clearly. There is no other alternative. We can't go back to the boat, and I know he's right as we both look up up up eighty feet above and realize that we have no idea where our dive boat is.

We are rookies in the darkness of these untried waters.

So, as we floated for these moments, suspended above this gaping mouth, I concentrated on merely breathing in and out, to regulate both my physical position and my stress. There's nothing else to be done. Larry won't go without me, and I won't go. It's easy to peer into the cave because we are hovering above it, still in some control of what we see and where we are, but inside it will be different. The blackness of the cave overwhelms – it's hopelessness and fearsomeness and silence are stronger than I. I will not go.

There is nothing here but silence.

Suddenly, from the cave mouth comes a silent surprise – the brown hand of the dive master emerges from the deep black, quick and ready, furiously shaking and grabbing at the water, searching for something. A lost diver perhaps, someone left behind, a coward or a novice swimming in waters way above her head, unprepared for the dark path that awaits even though she had been told that it would come. The master's quick hand was searching for the person who would not, could not follow him into the darkness.

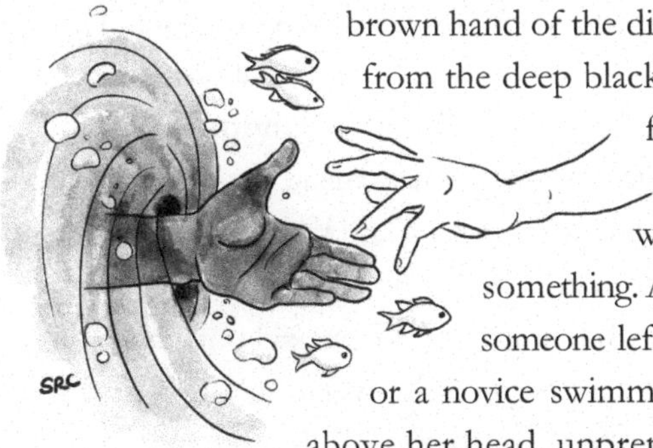

What will happen if I take the hand of the master, do I dare? There was odd beauty in this silence, quite unexpected.

I'd like to think it was an act of faith, but really it was just a lack of options that made me exhale enough breath to lower my scuba-clad-self close enough to the reef mouth to take his hand. I reached out, I did, but the dive master reached harder and with more deliberation and the instant his fingers touched mine, he grabbed my hand with the power of a great sea creature and pulled me into the inky, pitchy darkness of a deep, underwater, black hole.

Where there was no light at all.

We swam blind in the dark for thirty feet or more. Thirty feet doesn't seem like much when one is walking off room dimensions or even swimming laps. But in the dark, it is slow-going. I think it was the silence that made the journey seem so very very long. Silent swimming and the blackness of such a place, what choice had I but to hold onto the brown hand of the dive master. Rather, truth told, he held onto mine with the firm grip of one who would never lose a diver in this darkness. He had been here before, and he knew the way. Together we moved through, together turned the corner.

I could see it coming, glimpses of blue light dancing on the rough cave walls in what still felt like a great distance away. Not really light, more like the thought of light. Is this what hope looks like? Is hope a thing to be seen? I wondered.

I blinked and squinted and blinked again, unsure but sure of one thing only, that I was doing absolutely none of the work of swimming – neither kick nor stroke – I was being dragged toward the promise of light and a glimpse of blue that can only be seen here, in this very spot and nowhere else on earth. I felt light brushes, tickles of something against my arm, and instinctively I glanced over my shoulder. In grand wonder I saw the glimmer of those neon fishes, thousands and millions and billions of them, more than the bright stars in the sky, flitting and dancing in great groups all around me, touching me, welcoming me, gleefully reflecting the greens and pinks and oranges of their creation.

Reflecting the light. Glory be to God for all these dappled things.

As promised, there it was. The minute we turned the corner, the dive master released his mighty grip and swam speedily on ahead of me; he had other divers to attend to. My instinct followed him. I swam. Within seconds I found myself out of the Black Hole and swimming back into the vastness of the sea itself, though at a much greater depth – we traveled down as well! – and looking into that heavenly blue that the master had promised. Look up and the water is so clear that, even at this depth, over 100 feet, I could see the whiteness of the breaking waves on the surface of the water. The sun shone brilliantly through and the water was light, then darker and darker blue. Look down and the waters darken to a blue unique to deep, deep water.

Blue far beyond meager words – marine and sapphire and royal and cobalt and midnight – nothing sufficient to describe the blue of an ocean depth where dark darkness mingles with light. Don't forget to look both up and down, the dive master had instructed. The dark blue water of the depths combined with the light blue water above you creates a color like nothing else on earth. It's like a heaven. That's why we go to the Black Hole, to see that blue, to know it's real.

What a gift the dive master gave me that day; he took me through the blackness, not around it or above it or below it but through it and I was never for a moment alone. And this I now know, that even in the deepest places, there is a hand in the darkness ready to take mine in my time of most quiet need. In my most desperate place, my most alone moments, my blackest holes – dug by myself or others, it matters no longer – the Master is there, hand outstretched, reaching, reaching. For me.

Thomas Dorsey, who, in 1938, wrote the old gospel song, *Precious Lord, Take My Hand*, understood this. Deep in us all, I think his words resound – *I am tired, I am weak…Lead me on to the light…Take my hand, precious Lord, lead me home.*

That's why we go to the Black Hole, the Caymanian dive master had said. You really can't see the bluest blue until you've seen the blackest black, that's all I know.

Sometimes our knowledge and preparation and personality and strength are just not enough. Sometimes the dark is too dark and the light is just too far away and we lose hope of ever seeing anything else but the inky blackness. The Master lives there too, hand outstretched, saying, Ah, all is good, mon, no worries. I'll be there with you.

Take my hand, precious Lord, lead me home.

If the auditions ever came close to her home,
she would try out, just for fun.

It's Been Real, American Idol

I sit in the stands of the arena at the University of Minnesota, up in the cheap seats. It's noisy here, even this high up. Below me, on the basketball floor, eight long tables stand strong along the length of the floor, flimsy cloth partitions between each of them. The guy with the bullhorn, one of the directors, is making constant announcements, but he's hard to hear for all around me kids are warming up – guitars strumming and pitch pipes humming, a young man vocalizing by the women's restroom, *mi mi mi mi mi*. He's pretty good. The bullhorn just called for Group One, her group, so down she goes toward the hard floor, toward the partitioned tables, her turn to audition for American Idol.

It's been on her bucket list. If the auditions ever came close to her home, she would try out, just for fun. So, when the auditions indeed *did* come within a few hours of where she lived, she called her mother. Mom, do you want to go with me to the American Idol auditions? Uh, yes, of course I do.

We arrive at the arena at 4:30 in the morning, dark still, cold even in the summer, and early enough to be at the start of the line. Being close to the front has advantages; for her, clear and close proximity to Ryan Seacrest during the countless promo-shots, surely one of these shots will make it to TV, right?! And for me, getting to go into the arena a bit sooner, a real plus as it has started to sprinkle and my umbrella is, as ever, back at the hotel.

We are not the only mother-daughter duo; in fact, I would guess that this is the most likely combination in this line. Molly and her mother stand beside us and quickly become our companions for the day, a bit like seeing old friends at a reunion. Molly is one of six children from a pastor's family, and her mother and I immediately discover how much we have in common. We talk church while the girls warm their voices with the organic sing-a-long that begins behind us, the Monkee's "I'm a Believer," a song from my era; I know the words and sing them, loud. Molly's mother is filming. I fetch bagels and coffee and waters for the group from the shop around the corner. Everyone is scoping out the competition.

I recommend a day of standing in line with one's daughter.

There are scads of kooks in a place like this, and the cameras love them. Local news is swarming, interviewing the talent and the kooks alike. The cameras particularly like the guy dressed completely in yellow – his suit, shoes, socks, shirt, top hat, all bright canary-yellow. The AI director with the bullhorn beckons him in particular when filming begins, hollering, Where's that guy in the yellow suit? You sir, yes, you in the yellow, could you come up here, close to the boom camera? They definitely want Mr. Yellow to make the promo shot. And then there's the guy who wanders throughout the line all morning, *screeching* his songs and banging on his guitar and bumping people with his weird little dance steps. Indefatigable, this one gets on camera at least twice.

I'm particularly fond of the production disclaimer posted everywhere, on easels that blow down all day long in the cool Minnesota breezes: the production may use any sound or gesture one makes, good or bad, any weird face, any rude comments (which, for the record, they try painstakingly to obtain), anything and everything one does on camera belongs to the production and (it really says this) may be used and viewed anywhere in the *universe,* in perpetuity. This is not their first rodeo; this disclaimer covers literally everything in the universe. They are acutely aware that there are kooks here, as well as future stars.

The bullhorn calls and off they go, Rainey, Molly, and the rest of their group, this lot of hopeful singing folk, down long stairs toward the basketball floor to tables where producers sit. They go to sing their songs and wait to be judged. That's how this stuff works. And all I can do is watch. Rainey tells me later it's not scary at all until you step onto the floor, then it changes, it becomes a real reality show. It grows quiet down there, on the floor, she says, no more warming up or happy group sing-a-longs. Maybe for the first time everyone becomes fully aware of what this is – a competition, an *elimination* competition – and everyone in line is now a competitor, even our dear lovely Molly. Only one will win, everyone else will be discarded. With every step one must muster a little more courage.

It's brutal out there.

In this first round, contestants audition in groups of eight. Group after group stands vulnerable before the elimination tables, one by one they sing, and so far no one has received the Golden Ticket, the first passage on the road to stardom. Not one, not yet. It feels ancient in here, gladiatorial in tone. As Rainey and Molly inch closer to the tables, a first shriek pierces the busy air; someone has finally gotten a ticket. Molly takes Rainey's hand and whispers hard her epiphany – *We really may not get through* – for the very first time grasping the fact that of the thousands of people lined up to sing their well-rehearsed thirty-second snippets, only a tiny handful will actually move on. Quiet, they wait.

When your turn comes, you stand before the judges in a line of four, the other four of your octet behind you. The producers quick-read your bio and take a look at your clothes, maybe they glance at your face. You've got thirty seconds. Someone says, Sing, and you sing. Then someone says, Yes, go through or No, good-by. Then it's finished, simple as that. You have thirty seconds to make it or break it.

It's rough out there.

Molly's mother and I sit high in the nosebleed section of the arena. We cannot hear anything but singers in other groups not yet called down to the floor, still congregating by the bathroom, warming up, laughing, not yet nervous. The bullhorn squawks. The hot dog stand is open for business. There are Cokes and hot chocolate. We can see our girls from this distance, but just barely. Molly steps forward to sing, and her gentle mother leans forward in her seat. We cannot hear a thing. Molly done, Rainey steps up and extends her gentile, Southern-bred hand to the woman producer who does not shake it. That can't be good. Rainey steps back to her place in the line and sings. She throws her head back, clenches her fists, and offers her sweet song to the savage universe. The group has done its best and now it is finished.

Not a one of them gets through.

I have disliked reality TV since its inception, quite sure that it brings out the worst in everyone and that it is, in no way, real. Certainly, we as a culture are nearing some new low when we sit to watch people speak *their own mother-tongue* so poorly that subtitles are required; are we really gathering on our couches to laugh and mock them? We cheer young women on to sleep with any number of men in hopes of finding, within a tight six-week production schedule, their soul mate. It's all so cringeworthily ugly.

I still think these things. But something real happens to me on this cold Minnesota day, watching those girls walk out onto the hard floor to stand before the judgment seat, watching that woman producer *not* shake my daughter's eager hand, watching so few get what they hoped for. It's a microcosm of this process called real life, and it's too often brutal.

It takes courage to go outside sometimes.

Molly's sweet, naïve whisper, *we might not get through,* is right. Sometimes we don't get what we want or even what we need. Not everyone makes it through, that is the reality of it. Sometimes forgiveness isn't sought, and sometimes it is sought but not given. That's real. I wish it were not so, but enemies exist in real life and sometimes things are not reconciled. In this life, we get the thunder *and* the sunshine. That's real. When push comes to shove, many people shove. They root not for us because they are rooting for themselves, and we are simply in their way. When the pressure builds, life is not always a happy sing-a-long.

And there are, indeed, a lot of kooks out there.

We have a text thread going throughout the day, keeping husbands and grandmothers and clutches of friends updated on all the developments in the pseudo-world of American Idol. All a little melancholy when Rainey doesn't go through, Nanny says it best in her text:

How many people would love to audition but let their fear stop them? It is better to have sung and lost than never to have sung at all.

Amen, Nanny, you got that right. We only have this one wild and messy life, and it's sometimes brutal out there. It takes courage to live it fully, even to try, and we only have today for who knows what tomorrow may bring? It takes courage to face an old fear, to scare an ancient skeleton from the closet, to leave childhood terrors behind, to try, and to embrace life today. It takes courage to try something you've always feared, some-thing messy and unpredictable, knowing full well it's a long-shot, just to know you tried. It takes courage to pursue a dream, whole-hearted, tight-fisted, jaw-clenched. To sing your unique song to the indifferent universe, come what may.

To not be afraid, to not be afraid, to try and try and try not to be afraid.

What if we changed the measuring stick? What if we measured our lives not in coffee spoons and reality television and the status quo, but rather in courage? What if finding the courage to risk again, to laugh again, to forgive again, to believe again, to try again, to sing again, to live again were the measuring rod – I could live with that.

The cup of courage is a paradox – it refills richer and deeper with every emptying. Do I dare to dig deep into the cup of courage and choose to love again, love hard through pain? To follow a wild dream?

Rainey dared, on that wild and messy Minnesota day, to give it all she had, to risk, to throw caution to cruel judgmental winds and against all odds to try, just try. Rejection is never the end unless we choose to let it be. My daughter walks back to the car without a single regret.

Now, *that's* real.

SOMETIMES THE CAKE FALLS

The best moments are never ever without struggle. I stood apart, against the far wall at the back of the room, in search of a quick quiet moment – just one! – only to find such a small thing difficult on a big day. I stood by myself beside the wedding cake to watch the couple dance their first dance – the cake and I had a great view.

Her wedding reception, planned and worked on for months. Tablecloths and tastings and flowers and lists, a hot summer-full of back porch sitting, listening to wedding music, finding just the right songs for the service and singing them together over and over, the three of us just days before it became the four of us and our little group grew even better, stronger. The best of times Dickens calls this, and it was here and now and I wanted to look at it and taste it and hold it tight and remember every detail. I'm going to miss this when it's over, but for now it is here and I am here and a wedding for an only daughter happens but once.

The cake and I took stock of the happy room and I thought to myself this must be a glimmer of what Heaven is like – people dancing and laughing and feasting together with no strife, no anger, not tonight. An evening for gladness, celebrating a bride and her groom. The cake agrees.

The Wedding-Coordinator met me at the back of the church even while the recessional music still filled the air and I was nothing but smiles. The wedding had gone off without a hitch, perfect music, lovely friends, happy bride and groom. It was just wonderful, wasn't it? I declared, setting down the small bouquet to slip my feet out of my too-tall mother-of-the-bride heels for a moment of relief. There was an odd pause from the Wedding-Coordinator. I need to tell you something before you get to the reception, she began, her clipboard twitchy in her usually stable hand. What is it? I asked, rubbing my feet, as it took her a long minute to say the words. The wedding cake fell down. All the way down, the top layer is on the floor, smashed.

A moment of silence for the fallen.

Good women got to work, that's what happens when things fall down. The caterer called the Wedding-Coordinator who sent her assistant to the reception venue to triage the situation, finally texting militarily from the venue, It's down, the cake is really down. The Wedding-Coordinator called the Cake-Baker who, tools in tow, U-turned her car in the middle of Poplar Avenue and returned to the scene of the accident to cry a bit and then get busy with reparations, strokes of new piped icing and flowers to hide the gaping loss that was the top layer of the wedding cake.

Why do these things happen? Who is responsible, who's to blame? These are the questions we ask, no, demand when things fall apart. It must have been the maintenance crew, last minute vacuuming, bumping the cake table, says the florist. It must have been the band and their big instruments, moving clumsily around the wedding cake, says the maintenance staff. It must have been this awful August heat, says everyone, hot as the Devil's front porch, simply too much steam for the cream cheese icing and heavy cake, too much heat, too little air-conditioning.

Not unlike my own mother's cake that also fell in its August to be refashioned and reformed by quick hands filled with immense love and Tinker Toys.

We always want to know why, don't we? Why things happen the way they do. And yet sometimes, most times, we cannot know. Things fall apart, the center cannot hold and things just crumble, fall down, get lost. Sometimes loss is not a disaster. Sometimes it is.

That relationship worked on so hard for years and years, but it takes two and only one remains willing. Forgiveness that is not sought, or worse, asked for but not given.

There are degrees of things, perspective. Loss has many faces. Sometimes children fall down, and sometimes buildings do.

Flat tires and flat lines are not the same. Every once in a while, we all find ourselves on the floor, smashed, broken, lost.

What do we do when things have fallen apart?

What happens *after* the cake falls?

This day the bride had the answer, what the cake already knew.

I caught her in the Sunday School classroom-turned-Bride's room just seconds before she was to run off to the get-away car in a shower of confetti. Beaming, glad-hearted, as happy as I have ever seen her. The Wedding-Coordinator said she would tell the Bride, but I knew I had to tell my daughter about her fallen cake. I need you to know something before you get to the reception, I began. Mother, is this not the most wonderful day *ever*?! she cried, giddy, unhearing. The wedding was perfect!

What is *perfect* anyway? I tell her that her wedding cake has fallen down. Is it bad, ruined? she asks. I don't know. I think so, maybe.

Another moment of silence for the fallen cake. Eye to eye, heart to heart, the bride spoke. Well, she said, let's get over to the reception venue and see what's next. After all, it's just cake, isn't it?

Sometimes, it is just cake.

Indeed, in every good story there is a hero.

What does a wedding cake look like after about half of it has slidden off the other half, smashed, broken? What does a *person* look like after the same thing happens? Different, changed. This cake looked nothing like its picture in the cake book. It had an entirely new aspect, a peculiar, eccentric beauty in its brokenness, the Leaning Tower of Pisa came first to mind. Half of it gone, hard-fallen on the worn carpet and whisked away by some crew I never saw. The original *fleur de lis* pattern replaced by quick, sweeping strokes of icing and extra flowers, the florist's quiet contribution. She was simply a different cake than she was before her fall. The baker and caterer had whisked her to the back of the ballroom and hidden her in a quieter corner where she and I now stood together watching.

After a long, hard afternoon, the cake finally spoke. I may be broken, the cake declared in her moment of existential crisis, but I am not dead, she shouted. I am here! I am here!

She survived her breaking, not dead yet. Here's the secret to brokenness, she whispered and I leaned in to hear. The grace is in the getting back up, in the restoration. Accept the help of any good folk who come alongside to fill in the cracks and breaks and make you into something new, better, stronger, more beautiful than before. Accept the grace of those who help instead of hurt and heal instead of destroy, for those folk are God's own hands and that's where healing lives and where grace dwells. Standing up again after utter devastation with the courage to believe you still matter, that God did not kill you but rather broke you in the crucible of his grace to use you in newness and in completely original ways, even if others have moved you to the back of the room.

The grace is in the breaking and in the changing and in the repair. One can stand again.

The cake was content, peaceful in her angle of lopsided repose. Like Jacob of old, walking with the limp of brokenness after his wrestling match with God – limps remind us there is strength after destruction if we can endure and not faint. Make no mistake, everyone limps, and those who don't seem to are either pretending or they hardheartedly disallow the brokenness – either way, they are missing the grace.

If I run from the brokenness, I run from the grace.

I know there were many guests that evening who wondered about this cake, talked about her behind her broken back and her toplessness. *This is kind of a short cake, don't you think* and *I wonder if there will be enough for everyone to have a bite* and *Did I overhear that this cake fell down?* There are always those who talk, who add insult to injury, who judge through their own limited lenses. Oddly, after such a complete collapse, the cake doesn't seem to care much what they think.

Imperfect beauty, eccentric and broken hard, then loved back into newness. I love this cake.

The cake and I stood together in this moment, one of the most memorable of my life, and we watched the tiny glimpse of Heaven unfold before us as in a mirror dimly. I have a fuller understanding now of why God chose a wedding feast as his metaphor for Heaven.

So, remember this. True beauty comes not in spite of brokenness but because of it. The cake reminds me of what I always seem to forget, that God in his grace sends bakers and caterers and caregivers and teachers and friends to the kitchens and emergency rooms of our lives and in their tool bags lay the gentle reminders that pain is the path to grace and brokenness is the crucible that burns us to perfection. The truly broken accept the beauty of the patching and the bandaging to walk forward in the strength and beauty of their own unique brokenness.

You are not alone. We all limp a little, whether we admit it or not.

Unleashed

I wake up early, sometimes too early. If the weather agrees, I wander out to my back porch, coffee hot in hand, to wait for morning's first light, a gentle blush of bluing pushing back the black as the sun's pink fingers greet the flat edges of the world and heat the furry tops of the tall, thin pines. I may take a little stroll to the top of the lane and listen to the sounds of sparrows waking and read a little and write a little and keep trying to master the art of Sudoku puzzles. My early morning stuff, often way too early.

On one particular hot summer day, we do something out of our ordinary. Dogs in tow, we head down to the river, the grand and mighty Mississippi that lives and moves and breathes its stories at the margin of our busy city. The river has been above flood level for much of the summer, banks bulging, waters running high and climbing over the trees and tall grasses of our riverside parks and flooding flooding epically flooding the rice fields of Arkansas just west of us. River currents are up and swirling hard and we come to witness wildness.

We walk by the river in the morning quiet, to see what we can see. No one much is out yet, only a few odd, early birds like us. Silent long-necked herons fly high overhead, three of them;

no wait, there's a fourth, almost black, moving slowly, ghostly across the brightening sky. Sparrows twitter and flit in girlish groups as they hunt and fish for breakfast, their morning work, and two white-chested hawks sit high, majestic and still on the stiff branches of trees standing proud even midst dark and heavy floodwaters splashing at their trunks. We join the hawks and sparrows and trees and watch the river and listen; all of us on her ancient wet banks long to hear her voice today, we've risen early for it.

I need to hear something new.

Near the river's edge a man stands tall and straight like the trees, his hands pressed together at his chest, right foot firm and strong at the top of his left thigh. When he moves his movement is deliberate, his discipline quiet and precise as he bends to place his hands on the damp morning earth, then stands again, his morning practice. Behind him, white tugboats push small islands upstream and down, muddy waters splashing wild against these long sluggish barges, lapping and teasing the impossibly heavy loads. What's on board today, what's your haul, beans or corn or cotton? I wonder. Steel or river rock or some kind of fuel? Does it matter to the boat what the load is? The regal tugboats are silent, content to do their job on all waters, low or high or still or rushing, tugs push their unknown cargo on to the next port and the next, and suddenly Tennyson words float across the whirring – *He works his work, I mine.* The strong barge knows his day's work and forges forward, happy, free to work this river.

The dogs love it here. Unleashed they run far and fast, parallel to the flow. River waters have overflowed their restrictive banks and so have the pups, running on tall splashy grass, jumping and barking with loud delight at the unexpected cool the water offers. Joe is the older and usually more cautious of the two, but today he runs wild and unusually free, galloping from the soggy shoreline up the steep levee and back way more than once, the stoic hawks in branches overhead eyeing him and nodding their approval. *Run wild* they tell Joe as they depart their morning branch to do the same. Andy, the pup, dares the rolling waters nose-first, gleeful at the grassy edges, water flying high with his every shake. Nose in again, he dives head-first into the morning, all morning long.

Everything at this river's edge is living in a grand moment of freedom – no thought of yesterday or tomorrow – and I want to do the same, to try. I stick my toes into the water and venture a last quiet look upstream before the morning gets city-noisy, and I spot a raft on the far side of the river, built of heavy logs, driftwood, and rope. Squinting, I can see two men aboard the homemade craft; no, it's a man and a boy, their long poles lunged hard into the swollen river, pushing forward, forward. They move with great purpose this morning, executing the boy Huck's grand plan of heading to Cairo, at the bottom of Illinois where the Ohio River comes in. There they plan to sell the raft and take a steamboat into Ohio, one of the free states, where the man Jim won't be in danger of being sold back into slavery. Their great desire is to live unleashed.

What Jim and Huck do not know is a critical element in the story, irony-intense; Jim is free already, the Widow Douglas died and freed him in her will. I shout this story to them across the river – *Jim, you are already free! You don't have to make this difficult journey upriver, come back!* – but the two cannot hear me for they are laughing there on the far side of the river, pushing north against the flow.

Only then can I hear the river's whisper, what hawks and herons hear as they fly over muddy waters, what the dogs remind me in their running and what the trees shout even as they stand firm in the midst of grand flooding. What Creation tells me if I am quiet enough, if I have ears to hear – that freedom is work, a constant struggle against bondage of self and others. It's a battle to become unleashed.

Perhaps the joy in freedom is the work it takes to get there and the extreme effort it takes to stay there, the push to return again and again and again to one's purpose. To roll the boulder up the hill and when it rolls back down – and it always will – to turn and do it again. Is it possible that in the turning, the choice, the effort, the accepting of the very limits of our own existence is the place, or at least *a* place, where one finds joy, and humanity, and purpose?

There is freedom in the turning, the placing of my hands back into the everyday hard work of being a human on this lovely planet, the constant struggle of loving and forgiving and pausing and listening and not speaking and practicing empathy and laying down anger and picking up love instead and setting prejudices aside and laughing and singing and wrestling every day and working working working for freedom.

The struggle is to become as fully human as the hawk is a hawk and the dog is a dog and the tree is a tree and the river is the river. This is my work, the freedom for which I daily grapple, for I know in the deepest place in my heart that's where the joy dwells.

The sun rises hot and white; summer in Memphis is a brilliant heat. The city wakes and begins her work. Pushing and pulling, we all make our way, trying to live unleashed, like the pups and the birds and the trees and the river.

This struggle is our story.

What a Stamp Costs

My goal for my summer break is always the same: to write more thank-you notes. A thank-you note every day or at least every week or at least every other week or at least a couple throughout the course of the summer. I mean to do it, I want to do it, I need to do it. I read books about intentional gratitude, and I try to practice thanksgiving in the words I choose to speak, but as miserable irony would have it, I fail in the practice of actually getting around to writing the notes, picking up a pen and pressing it to paper in the name of gratitude.

Last summer, my plan was to write a handwritten note every day, a worthy goal for a writing teacher out of school and a lover of the written word and a practitioner of the art of lovely handwriting for the sake of itself. On the first official Monday of summer, though, I, uh oh, predictably, um, well, did not write a single note, not one kind or thankful word scribbled onto a page, no, not one. I sat in the sun and read my book instead.

Day 1 of summer, a gratitude and writing disaster.

Day 2 of summer, the guilt from Day 1's epic fail urged my pen to paper, and I cranked out two thank-you notes and was immediately flooded with the grand satisfaction that springs from accomplishing a goal, albeit a small goal, but at once I felt better about myself as a human being and began looking through my kitchen drawers for a reward. I felt worthy of love and acceptance, and my steadfast place in the whole of humanity was once again secured. Hoorah, I am saved!

But then, of course, I couldn't find any stamps. I normally pick up stamps at school, so searching my house for them felt a bit needle-in-a-haystack-y. I pushed into drawers unopened since we moved here (nine years ago) and looked at the bottom of my sock drawer (don't ask me why). I even cleaned and sorted out the glove compartment of my car and wondered for too long why we still call this space a *glove* compartment when nobody (at least no one I know) still places gloves into this small space.

My searching was not for naught, as I finally uncovered a couple of sheets of Santa stamps under a pile of last year's Christmas cards. Hallelujah, these thank-you notes may actually be mailed – a Christmas miracle indeed. Except for the fact that the Christmas stamps were 33-cent stamps. It dawned on me at that moment that I had absolutely no idea the current cost of a stamp these days. None. Embarrassingly I had to Google it – 58 cents! Stamps cost 58 cents apiece! This is hard to imagine, that's a lot of cents.

Now what? I had two thank-you notes written and ready to mail and two stamps that were 25 cents under the necessary requirement as mandated by the Postmaster General. I actually considered this dilemma for far too long before I reached my conclusion. Heck, I'll just take these over to my friends' houses and stick them in the mailboxes myself, it won't take long, they both live close by.

Only then did it dawn on me that I could simply place two 33-cent stamps on each envelope and avoid getting into my car entirely, though, I must say, this idea did *not* appeal to me. This plan was wasteful, with far more postage than necessary to get a card from here to there, 8 cents over cost. Isn't that extravagant, don't you think that is simply too much?

A friend of mine was once accused of having "too much grace." I have thought about that statement for years now, pondered what the speaker could possibly mean in accusing someone of having too much grace.

I wonder if anyone said that about Christ as He stood dying on the cross while at the same time praying for his murderers – Father, forgive them for they don't know what they are doing. Could it be that someone at the foot of that same cross, some mocker full of pride and chock-full of scorn said, That Guy just simply has too much grace.

Maybe someone did say that.

I wonder if anyone said that about Christ when the Pharisees, heavy stones in their eager hands, so ready to judge, so ripe to stone, brought to Him a woman caught in the act of adultery, and He forgave her and said, Go and don't do that anymore, you'll be so much happier if you can stop doing that. Could it be that one of those righteous Pharisees said, That Dude has too much grace, we're going to have to do something about that. Yes, in their anger and their strident fear and their jealous confusion, one of those stone-throwers may have said something just like that.

I wonder if anyone said that about Christ when He taught that we should forgive our enemy not just seven times for the same offense, but seventy times seven. Ridiculous, absurd! Could it be that someone in the crowd that day said, That is preposterous, no one could do that, no one *should*, no one deserves *that* much forgiveness. That Guy just simply teaches too much grace, He's nuts. I feel quite sure that someone said something like that.

Too much grace is like too much postage – it is lavish, way more than is necessary and way more than we deserve. No wonder people call it ridiculous and excessive and implausible, no wonder they cannot believe it, even when they see it – especially then. 66 cents when only 58 is necessary. What's this world coming to?

But is this not the very definition of grace – more given than is needed, more available than is asked for, or even dreamed of. Grace is free and no matter what anyone tells you, you can never have too much of it. And the good news is that there is plenty more where that came from.

Day 3 of summer, and I will be doing my best to hand-write notes this summer, notes full of thanks and love and hopefully pages and pages of grace. Then I will put stamps on these notes and mail them, even if I use up all the 33-cent Christmas stamps and have to get up out of my lawn chair and trudge over to the post office (which is right around the corner from my house) and buy more.

For I have learned that in the matters of the heart and soul, there is *never* too much grace.

Who is my Neighbor?

What lurks deep and lies quiet behind the masks we put on, behind the faces we prepare to meet the faces we will meet? I wrote this question in my journal a while back, intrigued by an admission from T.S. Eliot's J. Alfred Prufrock – pitiful, tortured, middle-class man. Fascinated I was and am with Prufrock's miserable, silent confession that, *There will be time… To prepare a face to meet the faces that you meet.*

Prufrock hates himself for donning a mask, for preparing his face every morning, but he goes through these motions nonetheless. Poor man.

Actually, I noticed the date in my journal and realized I jotted this question down over a hundred years ago, a hundred years before March 2020 when the whole world put on masks and I found myself teaching poetry online to eager high school students who definitively preferred discussing poetry in my cozy classroom with the twinkle lights over discussing poetry online at home, even if these scholars found themselves sitting outside in the sunshine or by the pool or eating breakfast or with the dog or especially with a little brother in the background who thought it funny to photobomb the Google Meet. My students, regular people yearning for the presence of one another, unmasked.

A hundred years ago I wrote that people don masks to hide their ugliness, to keep the secret things inside, covered, pressed down way down – prejudice and fear and hostility and enmity and foolishness and faintheartedness, and the hate that so easily besets me – and with a proper mask I can better forget hide ignore misremember disguise what lies within me hidden secret covered unrevealed, despite the myriad mirrors that surround.

A century ago, I thought wearing a mask, then metaphorical, was a given, conventional standard ordinary and normal. "Preparing a face" is of course the most vital *accoutrement* of my morning ablutions, for no one wants to see anyone's weak selfish critical fearful blotchy fragile skin.

So, in true Prufrockian fashion, I prepared my face, I put on my mask.

Preparing a face to meet the faces allowed me to appear to be better than I know I am, to be socially acceptable, to appear seemly by keeping unseemly things undercover, to look like the other faces that I meet, to fit in, to conform to concede to accede to concur to cooperate to comply to belong to protect to shield to be in line with to acquiesce to oblige to assimilate to peacemake to adhere to to accommodate to indulge to please to advance to benefit to defer to suit to satisfy.

The infinitives are infinite.

And now, these hundred years later, I understand the flip side, that wearing an actual mask does the same thing from the outside in. Now you see me, now you don't.

I don't mean to make excuses, but I do have compassion for us. So often we cannot see our own uglinesses for somewhere along the path our views became skewed, we believed a falsity and our mirrors bent (except perhaps the rear-view ones). We quite forgot our own vices for their presence became part of us like sunspots or freckles or moles or hair on our vulnerable bare backs. In a mirror at just the right angle with some exertion and effort, we can bend ourselves enough to take a quick look and examine what's going on back there, but most of the time such self-examination requires too much effort. And it's tiresome. And it hurts – and we hate hurt.

Not to mention, the effects of ugliness are easier to see in other faces. It is much simpler to look outward than inward, no personal twisting or bending required.

On the other side of all this maskedness, though, live millions of characters in the vast landscape of literature – the great reflecting glass – who understand their own ugliness and simply don't care.

A thousand years ago Shakespeare wrote *Othello,* and in the enormity of irony, on the very day I sit to write this essay the villain Iago showed up on my newsfeed.

This Iago is quite a guy, a man who knows his ugliness and enjoys it, loves it, declares it right out of the gate, and that is this: his proud and profound hatred for the *other*. *I hate the Moor*, Iago declares in his first soliloquy, his first time on stage by himself and we get the unmasked truth; the white Italian guy Iago hates the black Muslim guy Othello.

At least he's honest, this Iago. He knows exactly who he hates and he spews his vitriol with proud glee, no hidden agendas, no masks for him. He rips off any pretense of disguising his hatred his bigotry his sectarianism his prejudice his presumption his dogmatism and slaps it right out on the Internet for all to see.

And see they do. Today he had over 320,000 likes. This kind is not alone, they find great strength in these numbers.

A million years ago someone wrote down a story about a character named Jonah, have you read it? It's the one about the odd prophet-of-God, a seemingly simple story about a man who ran from God and ended up in the belly of a fish. (NOTE: If you've been to Sunday School in the South or anywhere near it, or if you have ever watched a Veggie Tale, you'll remember).

I wonder if that ancient man understood what landed him in a fish's belly in the first place, or if he ever admitted to himself why his story ends with him pouting under a dead tree, an angry and embittered man.

Did he, like Iago, realize his own hate?

Was he, like Iago, proud of his disdain?

One day long ago God's Word came to the prophet Jonah: *Arise, go unto Nineveh, that great city, and preach unto it the preaching that I bid thee.*

Jonah, who hated the Ninevites with the fire of a thousand suns, hopped up and ran in the exact opposite direction as fast as those feet would carry him; he hired a boat to Tarshish, heading as far away from God's voice as possible.

This story rests in our Western consciousness, I think. Man hears from God, Man runs from God, a storm comes and overwhelms Man, Man cries out to God, and God sends salvation.

I want to know more, though; I want to know *why* is Jonah running.

Turns out his is not a simple story about a whale.

Hatred and animosity and bigotry and condescension – uglinesses which some of us choose to mask and some do not – are certainly not original ideas. From the first moment Cain chose jealous anger, picked up violence and killed a brother, we humans have followed suit, donning anger and violence and cruelty as protective outer-garments. Swords and guns and words do their nasty work today as they did yesterday and sadly will do tomorrow. Hate and scorn-of-others have been around since the dawn of time, since the fall of angels, since a serpent arrived in a virgin garden.

This prophet-of-God named Jonah was a man, fallen like any other, and he ran for one simple, uncomplicated reason; he hated, loathed, nay, despised the people of Nineveh so dramatically that he was repulsed at the thought of their redemption. Glad he would have been if God simply doomed them all to hell and beyond, for he thought they deserved it for all the grief and agony the Ninevites had brought upon his people.

So, Jonah hit the road full speed ahead in the opposite direction. If anyone must bring the Ninevites a message of love or hope, it would not be him. He simply would *not* be a part of offering grace to an enemy.

Why such hatred?

Nineveh was the capital city of Assyria, Israel's bitterest enemy, and Assyria had enslaved Jonah's people for decades. Jonah grew up with the stories of the wretchedness of the Assyrians, he felt the weight of Assyrian oppression so burdensome that Israel became but a shadow of her former self, and he himself became a man living in the dark shadow of the slavery of his people. Year after horrible year, Jews were captured and deported as slaves to Assyria, forced to build Assyrian canals and foreign temples.

God asked Jonah to deliver a message of Grace:
Repent, and disaster will not befall you.

Assyrian art reveals headhunters with piles and piles of heads at their feet, quite accomplished they were at their hunting, men impaled on spikes, heaps of noses and hands and ears cut off for mere sport, the art of skinning and beheading their forte.

God asked His prophet Jonah to deliver a message of love and redemption to Nineveh, to these *uber*-violent Assyrians, a message of mercy to the very ones who murdered Israel's babes and raped her women and maimed and beheaded and killed her men.

Yet God asked Jonah to deliver His grace-message – *repent, and disaster will not befall you.*

Messages of grace and mercy seem decidedly unfair when God offers them to those we hate, and Jonah wanted no part of this sort of grace, had no interest in being grace's vehicle to these murderous barbarians.

So, he ran. He hired a boat.

Soon though, a hurricane cyclone typhoon of enormous magnitude rose up in the sea and nearly destroyed the boat, and Jonah found himself sitting in the belly of a great fish (a whale?) for a few days.

But on the third day of Jonah's cetacean cruise, the fish spit Jonah out onto the beaches of Nineveh, the very beaches from which he ran.

Somewhere, somehow, eventually the message of grace finds its audience.

Nineveh was a big place, a thriving city of 120,000, one of the largest in its day. Jonah trod angry amongst his direst enemies, probably looking quite worse for wear, digestive juices having played their untidy role. He likely had no hair left, lips and skin bleached white as snow, eyelashes and fingernails vanished.

What a sight.

Did Jonah, walking the tawdry streets of Nineveh, see his enslaved countrymen working under the whip of the mighty king? Did he witness grand Assyrian temples being built by the sweat and hands of Jewish slaves?

I think he did.

Did the prophet seethe with loathing great and rage hard at both the Assyrian people and his required task among them?

I think he did.

Did he hate the Assyrians even more for what he now saw with his own blurry, sea-drenched eyes?

I think he did.

These Ninevites, heartless, murdering barbarians, did not deserve the grace of God, of this Jonah was sure. Yet, the belly of the fish still quite fresh on his skin and in his mind,

Jonah delivered the message he had to and then hobbled from the heinous city as quick as his scaly feet would carry him.

Jonah began to enter into the city a day's journey, and he cried, and said, Yet forty days, and Nineveh shall be overthrown.

In a surprise turn of events, the King of Nineveh heard Jonah's message and feared the God who sent it. Throwing off his royal robes, the king sat down in the dirt and told all his people to do the same – *Everyone must turn around, turn back from an evil life and the violent ways that stain their hands. Who knows? Maybe God will turn around and change his mind about us, quit being angry with us and let us live!*

And the God of mercy and love did change His mind, this One not willing that any should perish.

One might think this pale prophet would be glad that his message was received by the King and his Ninevites. But not this prophet; this one fumed at the salvation of his enemy and stomped out of town, livid.

Sitting alone and pouting under a large gourd vine, Jonah heard of his enemies' repentance and he grew in rage and fury with each moment that passed. *I knew it,* he moaned and groaned and wailed in petulance at God, fists and jaw clenched tight. *When I was back home, I knew this was going to happen! That's why I ran off to Tarshish! I knew you were sheer grace and mercy, not easily angered, rich in love, and ready at the drop of a hat to turn your plans of punishment into a program of forgiveness.*

There it is. Jonah demanded of God justice and punishment for his enemies, but God in his mercy provided forgiveness and mercy. This little story concludes with the prophet sitting alone in sullen petulance under a dying vine. What an odd man, this Jonah, this demander of justice; what a bitter, lonely, angry little man.

God's message is remarkably simple, summarized in one succinct sentence: *Love God and love your neighbor.*

Who is *my neighbor?* demanded the petulant prophet in his anger. To please God, whom do I *have* to love? A good question too often asked, with an answer I don't care to hear.

Petulance, it seems, is the opposite of grace.

Hate and superiority and cynicism are blood brothers, fierce and strong and difficult, almost impossible to defeat. Clothe these fraternal triplets with masks of disgust and derision and ridicule and scorn and we've created ourselves a powerful potion, a mighty, killing draught.

The reason I do not love my neighbor is because I do not *like* my neighbor. I find his views offensive and therefore worthy of my scorn, a fine fit for my hatred.

My neighbor does not deserve my love or grace of any kind,

so I cancel him. I understand this reasoning. But to commit to this world view, I must agree with Jonah.

I do not have to love my neighbor because...well, my neighbor is a racist a republican a Catholic a lesbian a socialist a democrat an atheist a Jew a Muslim a cruel mother a trans person an Evangelical a fascist a communist a Black person a Fox News viewer an immigrant a Nazi a liberal a gay person a person who drives too slowly in the left lane a white person an absent father a straight man a difficult boss a brown person a conservative a CNN News viewer a poor person a rich person...

This list, this list, this list, I'm so weary of this list that seems never ever ever ever to end but rather grows like kudzu in the deep hot South by leaps and bounds because, by God, we water the stuff every day!

My God, my God, when will this cycle end?

But but but . . . But what about *my* neighbor, you know that wretch, that one who stands against everything I stand for, the one I am free to hate and therefore hate him I will, with great gusto and shouts of glee! We holler in the streets and wave our hand-made placards with no idea (and no ears to hear) what actually frees us from our slavery of hate.

It's Grace.

My God, my God, will I even try to take off my mask-of-goodness-and-self-righteous-rightness? Do I dare to love somebody on this ever-growing list, to even try?

Only by Grace.

Grace opens her doors to all us wicked broken beggars who need salvation from our enormous love of scorn, salvation to love those we love to hate, salvation from the self-destruction of mind and body that enslaves us.

"What lurks deep and lies quiet behind the masks we put on, behind the faces we prepare to meet the faces we will meet?" This was my question, and the answer is, I don't know. Only this one thing I do know: I can change absolutely nothing around here, except myself, and that alone will be the sole focus of my work for my remaining days.

It is enough.

So today I'll try to lay down a few masks (my anger my hatred my prejudice my arrogance my condescension my bitterness my fear my judgment – *my God my God*) and take a good long look in the reflecting pool.

I'm too dang tired to do anything else.

A Thing With Feathers

A new friend of mine is a bird-lover like I am. Well, to tell the truth, my friend is a true bird-*lover* while I am more of a bird-appreciator, a faithful watcher, a food source, and I think precise nomenclature is important here because my friend's actual love for his backyard birds raises me up, reminds me of higher flight-paths, and causes me to want to do the same.

For isn't that what love does, offers us a better story?

A few weeks ago, my ornithological friend sent me a video of a young blackbird who recently arrived at his feeder, and the text describes this 'young pirate with a broken foot dangling pitifully under him.' As the days pass and my friend watches the story unfold, the bird's little broken foot finally falls off, and the now one-footed blackbird feeds at my friend's back porch every afternoon.

'He's the only blackbird not afraid of me,' my friend reports.

Wait. You mean to tell me that of all the birds in this entire backyard-blackbird congregation, only one is unafraid of the man providing the feast, only one little beast stands fearless – on his one foot and one stump – before the kind hand that feeds him.

Our little blackbird understands resilience.
His brokenness demands it.

Like those ten lepers in the Gospels, the ones Christ healed, yet only one returned to give thanks.

Oh, I love this bird.

A few days later I ask for an update on the broken bird. In the follow-up video, I can see the blackbird is faring well, he feeds and grows and flies without struggle. But the words that follow drive me to my knees in their lovely, easy truth. My friend reports in his text, 'This bird is clever, too. He's figured out how to balance himself by fluffing up his tail feathers or by placing his stump on a rock when he bends over to feed on mealworms.'

Of course he's figured it out, what grit! I wonder if this young hero doesn't have a mother-bird like mine with a voice of strength and resilience, a wise one who takes what comes and then says, I don't need to hear any excuses, go outside and figure out how to do what you need to do.

One thing I know for sure, our little blackbird understands resilience – his brokenness demands it. He's like my pliable crepe myrtle trees who often bow their tall heads all the way to the ground during the chaos of a violent spring storm or under the weight of winter's ice. My crepe myrtles bend low, but rarely break.

Neither does Sisyphus, my favorite myth, a man who turns and rolls his boulder up the mountain again and again and again, his back bent under the weight of his fate, but not broken. And at the end of the story, we are urged to consider Sisyphus happy. Imagine that.

Or like my friend Scott who has been in a wheelchair since high school – a boating accident – and yet when I saw him the other day at a Mother's Day event at Kirby Pines retirement community where both our mothers now live, and I asked him how he's doing, Scott replied without pause, Better than ever.

Resilience and her cousin persistence walk hand-in-hand at the edges of hope and wave their short arms and footless legs at the future in what must be something akin to joy.

Bent, but not without hope.

Emily Dickinson says it well, always: *Hope is the thing with feathers - / That perches in the soul - / And sings the tune without the words - / And never stops – at all –*

But wait, there's more. I watch my friend's bird videos more times than I'm willing to admit, but it isn't until my viewing numbers are in the triple digits that I finally see the beautiful part – I see the love. Somewhere between the first video and the second, I notice that someone (my friend? his lovely wife?) has placed a small stone beside the mealworms on the back porch railing, a stone on which the young bird can balance himself and rest his stump as he feeds.

Oh my, but is this not the essence of love, to make another's life easier, assuage his pain, help if we can. Love, if we can keep our eyes open, takes our breath away.

Love is no mere feeling that flits and fleets like a hatchling on thin, shaky legs. No! Love is active, so compelling and patient and kind that those fortunate enough to live and work within the orbit of a person who truly loves are drawn upward, to the very edge of decision: ignore love and turn from it, or pursue and embrace it. Make your choice.

My friend loves his little broken, backyard bird. He doesn't care that the bird is imperfect; in fact, I'll bet he finds the bird's thin black stump his most beautiful part.

I know I do.

I'd like to sit by my friend's lake and watch that footless bird; maybe I will one day. I'll wave my short little arm and hand at him and he'll wave his stump right back, just like that short-armed, fingerless man from England did in the fudge line at Bass Pro all those years ago.

The truth is simple enough. This lovely blackbird will never grow another foot, nor do we want him to. Perfection is overrated and exhausting while gorgeous imperfection and the community of the broken can be so full of life, as blessed irony would have it. I'll be surprised by imperfection no more, but rather delighted by it.

I've made my choice. I'll try.

ACKNOWLEDGMENTS

More than thanks to the family and friends and writers and poets who added wisdom and fun and deep gladness to the stories of my life. For the folk from Memphis to Virginia to East Tennessee to Texas to Mississippi to Belgium and back home again to Memphis who shared and continue to share their tales of joy and woe and awe and wonder, folk who have given me a full life filled with friendship.

For all the teachers who showed me how to be comfortable in my own skin and taught me to love reading and writing.

For St. Mary's Episcopal School where I have learned more about life and literature than I did in college (why was I in such a hurry back then?).

St. Mary's, a place where I belong, a place where the blood-sweat-and-tears of the martyrs – the Sisters of St. Mary's – still rings and sings in love every day throughout those hallowed halls. I believe in Constance and her companions; to continue the work they began, to add even a smidge to the legacy, is worth all the effort. It is work I love.

For Sheila Patrick who sang 'Amazing Grace' once with me in chapel and then, years later, introduced me to Cranston 'Rip' Coleman, a publisher who believed in my writing and stories and had the know-how to do something about it.

For Christ Community Church who loved us through.

For Penny and Eric, my brother whose antics and wit deserve a book of their own, who remembers all the stories differently than I do, with a brother's twist. A man who takes care of things.

For Rainey and Coleton and Teddy who bring me the joy and the smiles of my very full life, every single day.

For Nanny and Geezer who taught us all what love looks like.

And for Lad who built me a back porch so that I can write and watch the birds at the feeder at the same time – the one who still makes me laugh after all these years.

INDEX OF POEMS

Made in USA - Kendallville, IN
99264_9798985029826
12.30.2022 1316